Back Street Brighton

photographs & memories

a sequel to
Backyard Brighton

QueenSpark Book no 22
2nd edition

contents

facing page: 93 Edward Street

Introduction

Back Street Brighton: photographs & memories: a sequel to *Backyard Brighton* is based on a collection of photographs, from Brighton Borough Council Environmental Health Department, of buildings most of which were demolished in the fifties and sixties. The Environmental Health Department have generously made the photographs available for this publication. The photographs were taken by the Environmental Health Department in the late forties or early fifties, 'principally to form a collection of records relating to clearance, and also for [departmental] use to demonstrate those features of unfitness upon which the cases for clearance were based, i.e. most of the photographs demonstrated elements of disrepair, dampness, poor lighting, ventilation and sanitary arrangements, and bad arrangement [generally]. The streets ... represent the last ... Clearance Area Programme which was undertaken before clearance became inappropriate'.

Few of the photographs include people; but as in *Backyard Brighton*, they were taken as a record of the buildings, not of their inhabitants. This is a collection of photographs of places not portrayed in the seaside postcard (though some of the buildings are delightful), so they will be as unknown to many newcomers to Brighton, as they would have been to tourists and many well-to-do residents in the town in the fifties and sixties.

QueenSpark Books and the Lewis Cohen Urban Studies Centre at Brighton Polytechnic formed a bookmaking team, comprising people who had worked on *Backyard Brighton* with some new volunteers. We chose photographs which showed the streets themselves rather than the backs of the houses, so that they were more recognisable to the people who remembered them. As a result of articles published in the Evening Argus and the Brighton & Hove Leader, people who knew and lived in the streets depicted in the photographs have written down or told us about their memories; we are grateful to them for having taken so much trouble. All have provided us with a close focus view of their lives just a few decades ago.

As in *Backyard Brighton* the inhabitants were united by poverty, but they were also united by the dangers and anxieties of the Second World War, and they built up strong support networks within the community to help them survive the rigours of their lives. Not everyone had extended families, but everyone had neighbours. The demolition of a neighbourhood is not just the destruction of buildings, it is also the destruction of a complex social support system. People felt that they belonged to an area of the town (a small collection of streets around their home), and everyone knew where that area began and ended.

There was surprisingly little improvement in housing conditions between Backyard Brighton in the thirties and *Back Street Brighton* in the forties and fifties, but the Second World War halted a rise in living standards. The photographs in this book are of houses which were part of the final large scale comprehensive slum clearance programme in Brighton. Although most of the buildings only survive as photographs, memories of living in *Back Street Brighton* are still very much alive.

4 Artillery Street (now Churchill Square)

Jubilee Street

Jubilee Street had hardly a building worth a second glance, but the substantial Crown Shades public house about half way along the west side looked the best. It had many large rooms upstairs, which the licensee let furnished, on a short time basis, to the lower members of the cast in the variety shows at the Hippodrome. The bar trade was not busy enough to make a living.

Next door on the south side was Bill Hansford's barber shop, and adjoining that was a garage with large blue wooden doors used for Panto's delivery lorries. Panto's was a wholesale tobacconist and confectioner with a warehouse at the top of Crown Street off Western Road.

The north side of the Crown Shades, numbers 19 & 20, was originally the site of the Crown Brewery, which no one could remember. Before the Second World War they were sale rooms used by Edwin Tully; he lived in St. George's Road and traded there as William Stead's Complete House Furnishers. In Jubilee Street he auctioned second hand furniture, probably obtained cheaply when customers bought replacements. A short-tempered person, he raved at everyone in the auction rooms with no intention of purchasing anything. He was friendly with Brighton's cheeky chappie, Max Miller, who lived in Burlington Street, near St. George's Road. Occasionally Max visited the sale rooms on Friday morning, and as he arrived at Jubilee Street in his Rolls Royce, there was uproar.

After the Second World War Messrs E Sinden & Bros, the undertakers, used the premises as workshops for making coffins on the upper floor, and garaging hearses at ground level. The coffin makers, who also acted as bearers and attendants at funerals, were extremely jovial, and seemed determined not to become unduly depressed by their sad vocation.

Number 21 next door was occupied by Dumbrell's, a small firm of builders, decorators and plumbers who seemed capable of doing any job at short notice. They were experts at clearing blocked drains. Removal of a manhole cover revealed a hole at least fifteen feet deep, with iron footholds embedded in the sides. During torrential rain a blockage sometimes occurred, the hole filled and overflowed all around. Dumbrell's men arrived immediately, waded through the filthy water, removed the cover and inserted long rods. Locating the hole exactly and clearing it at that depth took time, but they never grumbled. Mrs Dumbrell lived nearby at number 1 Robert Street, and the family firm had traded in Jubilee Street since 1910 or even earlier. She left the running of the firm to her son-in-law Bill Hilton, an extremely pleasant person. He was churchwarden at the Chapel Royal where he was held in high esteem.

On the east side of the street between North Road and Shoesmith's yard were a few premises including a grocery shop run by Mr. Dudeney. Shoesmith's open yard had the main corn merchants premises at the far end. Both sides had lock-up stores or stables on the ground floor, with dwellings above. There were two on each side, reached by climbing outside wooden steps on to a wooden platform with a railing that gave access to the front doors. The dwellings must have been small, probably had mice, and were a fire risk with straw and hay all around, and possibly underneath. Tommy's cafe was on the outer corner of the right hand side of the yard.

Jubilee Street: (off Church Street) courtyard giving access to 29-34, east side

Walter and Lynn's premises were in and around the next yard to the south, which had a name, Old Farm Place. John Walter also owned the houses on both sides of the entrance; numbers 36 to 38, and 41 to 44. They were sold, I believe, when he died about 1943. The houses had three storeys, but the rooms were small, as were the back yards. The premises of Shoesmith's, Walter & Lynn, and Marsham's all extended and joined up behind the houses. Len Smart, who worked at Walter & Lynn in the bacon department, lived at number 44 at one time. The firm had three well-built brick bacon stoves, each capable of smoking one hundred and twenty sides of bacon, or even more if absolutely necessary. During one August week they sold over one thousand one-hundred sides of smoked bacon.

Before the Second World War George Newman & Co occupied numbers 45 to 47, a large garage building. Newman's specialised in high-class cars, with a sale room between Pool Valley and the Royal Albion Hotel, now a solitary building linked to the hotel. After the War Newman's garage in Jubilee Street was used by various firms and eventually taken over by Marsham's who traded in old tyres. New tyres were difficult to obtain in the 1950s, so old tyres were often retreaded. I am uncertain whether they retreaded them there, or used the garage as a store only.

We now come to the bottleneck. Jubilee Street suddenly narrowed, so that one shop in which secondhand dresses were sold, faced along the street. There was a small confectionery shop run by Albert Small on the eastern side of the bottleneck. Sweets were rationed up to the early 1950s, and Albert seemed to obtain a wider variety than most other shopkeepers. People made a point of calling there when they had unused coupons. Also on that side King, Thorne & Stace the printer had offices, with their workers almost opposite.

Near the Wagon & Horses on the corner of Church Street was a yard, once known as the Palace Yard. It was secure with a high stone wall on the Jubilee Street side, and a high wooden door completely enclosing the southern end. There was a variety of firms inside but I can only recall two. Arnold & Marshall were motor-body builders. Some firms needing a lorry ordered a chassis only from the makers, and arranged for local firms to build the body to individual requirements. Wyatt & Sons Ltd were dairy farmers with milk rounds. Crates to hold milk bottles were made of metal and sometimes required repair and welding. Wyatt's carried out that work in the yard.

The west side of the bottleneck was mainly taken up by the gloomy grey wall of the Central School; it was about fifteen feet high, with a short space above to provide air to the playground on the other side of the wall. That play area was covered by upper storeys. In the mid-fifties some classes played outside in Church Street at about one o'clock. Barber's Restaurant was on the corner at one time, but I cannot recollect when it was demolished. The bottleneck was finally made one way, north to south.

I don't know when the rot started, so many years have passed. I remember that it crept slowly all through Jubilee Street until every building and all sign of life disappeared. In the mid-fifties the houses numbered 36 to 38, and 41 to 44 had their windows boarded up by the authorities. The floor boards were removed to deter squatters, and even the doors were padlocked. It was said that the Medical Officer of Health had declared the houses 'unfit for habitation', and compensation of fifty pounds per house had been agreed.

I entered one of these houses on one occasion, and saw the ground floor. The front room was well papered, but the back room walls were uneven and cobbled, so they were whitewashed. The lady tenant kept the place spotlessly clean. As a small town house in Central Brighton it would fetch a high figure today.

Bill Hansford in his barber shop had a visit from the Medical Officer of Health or his representative, who received a hostile reception. It was soon deemed to be unfit for habitation and it was rumoured that a figure approaching one thousand pounds had been agreed. The Crown Shades was vacated, and squatters moved in upstairs. Opposite, a burglar broke the padlock door of number 41 and stepped over the floor joists to get into the back yard. From there he climbed a wall, walked along the lower edge of Walter & Lynn's glass roof, and forced open an office window.

Walter & Lynn received numerous letters about vacating the premises and moving elsewhere. One required a decision as a matter of urgency, as redevelopment was expected to begin in the near future. Thirty years have passed. The firm ceased trading in 1964 and the premises were demolished in the same year. An illustration in the Evening Argus dated 8th September 1964 shows the operation in progress and the caption read 'in readiness for road widening and a future conference hall'. They certainly got the road widening part right, Jubilee Street is the widest road in Brighton. The inside wall of the third bacon stove can still be seen, but the smoke exit above it is a relic of an older stove once used by Stewart's, another firm of provision merchants who traded in North Road and closed there about fifty years ago.

By early 1965 all the east side of Jubilee Street, between the backs of the shops in North Road and the bottleneck, had gone. A chainlink fence and a padlocked gate, about six feet high, were erected along the line of the old frontage, leaving the pavement for pedestrians. Motorists paid for a car bay and a key to the gate. Some businesses still held on into the 1970s; the funeral directors Sinden's were listed in the 1974 Directory at numbers 19 & 20, and Dumbrell's at number 21. In the Palace Yard at the other end of the street, the motor-body builders previously owned by Arnold & Marshall had been taken over by Mr A Collins, who had worked there for many years. Two other occupiers in the yard were also listed.

Facing the north end of Jubilee Street, in North Road, were five business premises. On the Kensington Street corner was a fruiterer's run by Edward Barker. Next down North Road was Luxford's Cafe, and adjoining that was a printing firm. Then came a baby linen shop run by Mrs. James. On the Robert Street corner before the Second World War stood the Noah's Ark, a small public house where Mr. Barden was licensed to sell beers only, not wines or spirits. There was little room in the bar, so when trade was good and the weather warm, some drinkers stood outside. Mr. Sallis traded there after the end of the war, the public house having been closed and converted into a shop. He stocked electrical accessories, including surplus items being sold to dealers by the War Department. Most were cheap, but you needed to be an expert to know whether it would suit your purpose.

Behind the shops, and stretching from Kensington Street to Robert Street were the premises of Collings & Aldrich, another firm of wholesale provision merchants with bacon stoves. About 1960 they ceased trading there, and at a later date the building and the five shops nearby were demolished. The Southern Publishing Company eventually extended up to North Road.

H L Dawes

I am seventy five years of age, and lived at number 36 Jubilee Street from 1917-1930, two doors from Shoesmith's, the corn merchants, who stabled their horses under the steps, though there were flats above. Six of us lived in the house; two sisters, two brothers, my niece, Mum and Dad and me. We had four bedrooms all partitioned with wood; if ever there was a fire we would all have been burnt to death.

I can't remember who our house belonged to, I think it belonged to Shoesmith's. We had a little yard at the back, concrete of course, and in one corner a furnace copper that boiled the water to do the washing. In the opposite corner the toilet, then a sink where you were supposed to wash, but of course we used to bring it into the scullery. There were no bathrooms; we went round the corner to the Public Baths in North Road, which was threepence; though when I was five or six I used to have a bath in a tin bath. I was about four I suppose when we first moved there, and I was about sixteen or so when we left. It was a very spartan sort of living. I used to go regularly every Monday morning as a boy to get half a bar of Sunlight soap, 2 1b of soda for Mum to do the washing and I had about a ha'porth of sweets, I think, out of sixpence.

There were a certain number of houses which looked as if they could have been shops, but they weren't; they had fixed windows instead of the sliding windows which we had. Then there was a builder called Dumbrell's, then another pub, the Crown Shades. They used to have a fight every Saturday night, mostly the women fought, not the men. They would be tearing one another's hair out, and you can imagine trying to hold them back! None of the houses had front gardens, but they had nice window ledges jutting out over the pavement, so people who were drunk used to sit on the window sill to sober up; my mother would go in the top bedroom and throw water over them. There was often a bit of a skirmish, but they were no bother to anybody; the police used to come up and stand at the end of the road, and it all used to die down. I remember one night my mum made a dreadful mistake; a policeman was having a rest on the window ledge, she thought it was a drunk so she threw water over him!

I went to the Central School in Church Street when I was seven, after Central Infant's School in Upper Gardner Street; it was a church school and so we had to march to St Peter's every week. They also marched to Brill's Baths in Pool Valley; and as the school had no playground they marched to Preston Park for games lessons. We also used to go to Circus Street for woodwork classes, that's how I became a carpenter and joiner for the rest of my life. They had a Sunday school at St Peter's Church, and we went on outings to Hassocks. We used to have to have a label tied on us to show where we were going! Can you imagine, just for going to Hassocks?

As children we played in North Place and made four-wheel trucks to go down North Road in the tram lines, much to the annoyance of the tram drivers. My friend lived in North Road, over a shop called Bennetts, and we used to play in North Place, a cul-de-sac between Jubilee Street and the main road. We had a metal hoop, and I used to go to school running like a hare round the corner of Regent Street. There were different seasons for toys which were popular, such as the top season.

One of the places we went to was the Coronation Cinema, which became Redhill Motors in North Road. In that part of Brighton you had everything you needed, we were never bored. We went down to the beach, in amongst the fish market, and collected crates of oranges when they were washed up on the beach.

Once we had all the rats come up in Jubilee Street. There was a wooden partition on the staircase, underneath the coal cellar. One day there was a terrific fight going on in there between the cat and a rat, and when they dragged it out it had been bitten quite a bit, but it had killed the rat. It was a big rat and they said it had come up from the drains. The whole place was torn to pieces after that and dug up to put a new drain into the mains. I don't think it really bothered anybody, apart from scaring my mother.

In Jubilee Street we had gas first, and then you could apply to the electricity works and they would wire your house for you; we eventually did that. I wanted to make the radio sets and all the rest of it, and if you could manage to get electricity you could do away with all these batteries you used to have.

My father, with his small business as a painter and decorator, did quite well, then we moved to a place in Hanover Terrace and that was the end of the business. Strangely enough, if you move, the business dies, because there weren't any yards like Shoesmith's to look after, and there weren't any other places to obtain work from. We were pleased to move from Jubilee Street into a bigger place, but it never really worked out, and I think we were happier in Jubilee Street than in the new place.

You left school at fourteen and started work. You never had any ambitions of doing anything except being a bricklayer, plumber or carpenter; we were trained to be craftsmen and that was that. I first started work at the age of fourteen in Sussex Street; wage five shillings, work eight in the morning to six in the evening, and eight to twelve on Saturday morning. I often had to push a hand barrow loaded with tools and ladders, there were no carts or lorries then. I was an apprentice to a place called Elliotts for four and sixpence a week in a joiners shop.

Everyone was friendly in Jubilee Street, there were one or two of the people who lived in what we called the posher houses who weren't quite the same, but everyone seemed to get on well together.

Leonard Smith

The photograph of Jubilee Street shows a courtyard which gives access to numbers 29 - 34 from the east side of the street. It would have been taken to show houses on either side with access up staircases, garages underneath and commercial premises; in other words mixed uses. The photograph was taken to demonstrate these mixed uses in the street more than anything else, and an unpaved front area with difficulty of access, and some sort of suspended walkways fronting the front doors.

Paul Eardley: Environmental Health Officer

Church Street

I was born at 41 Windsor Buildings in 1924. Windsor Street runs between North Street and Church Street, and the Buildings were a large block of flats near the North Street end. Number 41 was a one bedroomed flat on the top floor, and there were about a hundred and twenty stairs to reach it; there was no lift. There was one room where you lived and cooked; and a bedroom and toilet. There was no bathroom, and you had to go to North Road Public Baths for a bath.

I was the oldest, and when my brother and sister were born we moved down a floor to number 39. There were two bedrooms and a large room with a gas cooker, range and sink; it also doubled as a bedroom. At the bottom of the Buildings there was a little old washhouse, where people would leave their prams as they couldn't keep going up and down the stairs with them. Nobody used it as a washhouse any more as it was so old, it still had copper bowls for washing. Most people did their washing in their small sink in their flat, although some people did send it to the 'bag-wash'. We had balconies outside the flats, and we would tie the line and hang the washing out. We also had chutes for our rubbish on the landing, to save us carrying the bins up and down.

Church Street was full of shops. Norman's the secondhand clothes shop was at the top, there was also another one for men's clothing but I can't remember its name. There was a cafe on the corner, and the Windsor Tavern was next to a little sweet shop. There was another pub called the Lamb Inn, but Brown's and the tailor took it over. There was a shop that sold medals, military stuff and china; and Hill's the butcher who had fawn tiles outside. There was a greengrocer on the corner of King Street, and in King Street itself was a baker where they made lovely cakes.

There was also a bicycle shop with a yellowish front, and two fish shops: Andrew's, and another one painted a horrible dark green, which stood on the corner of Gerrard's Court. Steele's was a secondhand sewing machine shop that was run by a little old boy and his son. On the corner of Jew Street was a chemist, and Ted's the greengrocer; Phil West sold winkles and shell fish, and I believe that it is still a shell fish shop today. There was also a Kosher butcher in this area.

There was a big Gothic building that I think was the Central School. It was a shame that it was pulled down, because they only used the land as a car park. After Preece's Buildings, there was a haberdashery shop, a chemist, and 'The Film Star Shoe Shop' where they had all the latest fashions. Dockerill's and Shackleton's, the fish and chip shop were up from this. As children we would sit on the steps of the Regent Ballroom, and watch the celebrities go in with their lovely dresses and fur coats. I didn't go to the Regent myself, but years later I became an usherette there.

Cynthia Russell

20 Church Street

Blackman Street

I was born at 3 Blackman Street in 1904. I was the youngest of six boys and my mother died when I was thirteen. My father and some of my brothers worked on the fishing boats, so they used to leave early in the morning and leave me to get myself up and to school, but of course I often 'played the rag' and went down onto the beach. The school board man would sometimes catch me and take me back into school for a hiding. I didn't learn much at school, because I didn't attend often, but I could forge a note from my father to say that I was ill and they never queried it. I had learnt to slant my writing the other way to my own; if they said that they were coming round to see my father I used to say he wouldn't be back until late, because I knew they wouldn't come then.

My father also worked on the lifeboat and would have to rush down to the beach when the signal was given. I often went onto the beach to try to find things washed up from those boats that were wrecked, although you weren't supposed to touch them.

My eldest brother was killed in the First World War. He had been an apprentice watchmaker at Lawson's in St. James's Street, and another brother was a prisoner of war. When my brothers returned from the war they found it difficult to get work and the house was very crowded. There were only two small rooms downstairs and two upstairs, with another tiny room in the eaves. We had an outside toilet in a small back yard, and an outhouse where we washed. My family had lived there for many years. I believe that my grandfather had owned it at one time, but it had been sold to share the proceeds between his family when he died; anyway we rented it when we lived there. Gradually my brothers got work, married and moved away. I used to get paid 6d to cook the Sunday dinner when my brothers were at home.

When I left school I had many jobs. Some I started on the Monday and left on the Saturday; mainly the errand boy type of job. We worked a 48 hour week and got paid on Saturday night, to make sure we turned up. Later I took labouring type jobs, but there was a lot of unemployment in Brighton during the twenties and thirties. If you were unemployed you got a ticket for your groceries and you had to go to certain shops; they came round to your house to check that you hadn't got anything to sell. You had to sign on the dole every day between half past two and three o'clock; after six weeks they sent you to the manager to see why you still weren't working.

I married Kathleen when I was twenty one and she moved into 3 Blackman Street too. We had four children who were all born there, and we only moved from the house as it was a redevelopment area. They got us out under false pretences, and the site where our house stood is still waste land after all this time. When we were expecting our first child we asked for help from the parish. Kathleen's mother had given us a lump of coal for the fire as it was so cold, so when the report was written it said we were not in need because we had a 'blazing fire'.

Alfred Harman

(During 1939 Alfred joined the Royal Air Force and spent most of the war away from home. Kathleen was left at home to look after the four children.)

Blackman Street: (North Laine) looking north

He volunteered, so I got less money to manage on than the families where the husbands had been called up. I had to go to work at the station unloading goods from the trains. Well, what else could I do? My mother had my youngest boy David, so I had to take him to St. Mary Magdalene Street first and then go to work. We loaded jam onto the train one day, and just as it left Brighton station a bomb hit it. We had to clear up this sticky mess when the surviving part of the train returned.

I must have looked poor and thin because they took pity on me at the station and allowed me to go home on Sundays at 3 o'clock, as they knew I had a family. The money I got for Alfred being in the Forces was such a small amount I would only draw it out once a month, otherwise it wasn't worth the effort. I had thirteen and a penny a week to support a family of four, so I changed jobs and went to work for Tamplin's brewery on Lewes Road, stacking beer barrels on the lorries. I only weighed 7st 8lbs, but a man showed me how to stack them without noticing the weight and I found that I could do the job easily after that.

My brothers became worried about me living in Blackman Street because it was so near the station, and they thought the station would be bombed. They helped me put a blackout up and I moved out to Carden Avenue with my brother and sister-in-law for one night, but I returned the next day because my sister-in-law didn't make us welcome. Carden Avenue was then bombed, so we would have been no safer. I moved in with my mother in St. Mary Magdalene Street for a while, but that area was bombed. We returned to Blackman Street and we all sat under the table when there was a raid, but my nerves became very bad.

We lost our boy Bert in 1944, not through the war, but we just found him dead one morning. They never told us what it was, but I think it was hushed up, because he caught something which they didn't want known. We went to the Army, Navy and Airforce Society for help with the funeral, but all they did was send an undertaker round who made the funeral costs just over what we had in insurance. We paid ld a week for a child in those days and there was a limit on what you could claim. We had to pay the balance off weekly for his funeral. So much for help.

The Blackman Street area was very busy, and many people worked at the railway works or the electricity generator; a signalman lived opposite us. When work had finished for the day the streets would be full of workmen going home. It was a very good area to have a shop in, as so many people passed by. There was every shop available in the area, you didn't have to go far. We had the Co-op and Marks and Spencer in the area at one time. The grocery boy would come to the door and ask for your order book and return with your groceries later that day.

In 1929 we had signed a petition to get electricity into our street, as you had to get a certain amount of signatures. Even with electricity we didn't have many luxuries in the house, and many people were glad when they were offered new council houses on the estates, with baths and hot water. We didn't qualify for a house as our children had grown up and married by this time, so we were left to nearly last to be rehoused. We were given a flat in Albion Street, but my married son and family who were living with us at the time didn't get rehoused. The area has never been redeveloped, and some people said that the council ran out of money and left it looking derelict.

Kathleen Elisa Harman

Photograph of Blackman Street:1962/63, Hudson's in the background of the photograph, was not part of the compulsory purchase order, only houses were in the CPO. The photograph shows houses which have direct access onto the pavement and with evidence of disrepair. The environmental health problems would have been inside the houses.

Paul Eardley : Environmental Health Officer

Cheapside

My grandfather bought number 44 Cheapside from the original owner in the late nineteenth century. There was a small kitchen where my father had a bath fitted and an outside toilet in the small back yard. Last year (1988) I obtained an improvement grant to convert the smallest of the three bedrooms into a bathroom.

My grandfather (Grover Hook) was an antique restorer with a workshop in Frederick Place. We had our milk delivered by Barling Bros on the corner of St Peter's Street and Ann Street, but my mother also had one pint per day from Mr Keay in Belmont Street, to keep in with him. We had our greengrocery delivered from Ann Street, our groceries delivered from Eltonton's at the bottom of Trafalgar Street in York Place, and the London Road Co-op delivered our meat. I was only allowed to play with the children I met at church, and there were streets where my mother thought it best that I did not walk along. I can remember people arriving at St Bartholomew's in carriage and pairs, but it also catered for the people of the area.

The whole area was full of little houses, many in St Peter's Street had been renovated and improved. There was a general feeling of resistance when the compulsory purchase orders came through. The Environmental Health Officer sent letters saying that the houses were unfit to live in, but by this time, the fifties, many of the houses had been bought and done up. They came to look at our house, but I think that the modern buildings on either side saved us. Belmont Street went first and the residents complained that they did not get proper compensation.

Initially I had a feeling of loss when the area was being demolished, but this was replaced by a feeling of light as they knocked down the buildings opposite. The area has changed now that it has not been developed at all, it remains to this day a rough car park for shoppers.

Dorothy Seymour

Wood Street

I was born at 29 Wood St in 1925 and lived there until my mother's death in 1947. I have many happy memories and can still remember our little house. It consisted of the front room which was the best room and seldom ever used except for special occasions. All the best furniture etc. was kept in there (and an aspidistra of course). The kitchen was warm and cosy, not very big but we were comfortable in it. We had an open coal fire at first, but this fell to bits in the end and the landlord replaced it with a secondhand range called a kitchener. It incorporated an oven as well as the fireplace, but the oven never cooked properly, and although large and really very unsightly, the warmth that the fire threw out more than made up for it. There were cupboards built in either side of the fireplace in the recesses, which came in useful, and although not airing cupboards they at least could ensure that all the washing done was kept damp free once aired. That was done with the aid of several lines strung across the kitchen. Mother would do the ironing on the table, then throw it over the lines. As we had no electricity we had to have flat irons in those days, which were heated up on top of the stove.

Now, to the scullery; that was totally a different kettle of fish, very cold and damp. The walls were bare, just whitewashed stone, and the floor was concrete. We had a copper in the corner and a little shallow sink, just the one tap, no hot water. We had a black iron gas stove, which had to be black leaded. Outside we had a small backyard, a brick wall separating us from next door. At the end just round the corner was the toilet, which had a plain wooden seat. There was always a spare candle and matches left there as we had no other form of lighting. The winter months were hard, there were times when you had to wade ankle-deep in snow to get there.

Upstairs we had two bedrooms, they were kept warm with small gas fires. If it was very cold then Mother would light the little black valor oil stove, as that was cheaper to run for longer periods. We had gas lighting all over the house, the gas mantles were very fragile and always breaking, and made a hissing noise when alight. Most of the houses were similar to ours although some of the end houses had a cellar.

We had two pubs in the street; the one on the corner of Cheapside was called 'The Crosskeys' and was run by Mr. Nevatt and his wife. On the other corner we had a cobbler and his name was Mr. Stokes and he was kept very busy; everyone had their shoes mended many times before finally discarding them. Just around the corner was our little general shop, run by Mrs Martin. You could get most things there, and just the required amount, everything was weighed up. In the centre of the street was another pub called 'The Cabinetmaker's Arms' but I can't remember who ran that one. At the bottom on one corner was Mr. Marchant's shop, buying and selling secondhand furniture, and on the other corner was Bowley's the Bakers, so we were well catered for on the whole, for one little street.

I can remember so many of the neighbours, the whole street was like one big community centre, everybody knew everybody. Steps were washed and pavements swept. Nobody locked their front doors during the daytime, there was never any need to. As far as I know the only problem in the street were mice. We all had our fair share of them; most families had a cat so they weren't too much of a problem. At times they did get the better of our cat, but on the whole, as did all the cats in the street, he would do a good job, and we weren't bothered too much about them.

Wood Street: (North Laine) - west side

I can't say any of us had a lot of money to spare in those days, yet we were all well fed and none of my playmates were ever in rags, always clean and tidy. I can remember now being sent to the infant school with a hanky pinned to my dress.

Our mothers seldom went to work, they only went out when they had to do shopping. Their days were spent cooking, mending and cleaning. I know my Mother used to make all my dresses, and nothing I liked better was when on a Sunday summer's evening she would dress me up and take me out to Preston Park to listen to the band.

Another visit I used to look forward to was to watch the blacksmith shoeing his horses. I couldn't understand why the horses never made any fuss, for with all the smoke from the red hot irons that were used on their hooves, it looked as if they were being burnt to death, but they would emerge quite happily with their new shoes on and gallop off quite pleased with themselves. There were a lot of horses in those days for delivery vans, and I can remember now seeing one poor horse one very cold winter's day, having waited so long for his master outside of a shop in Sydney Street, unable to move, his feet frozen to the ground. The blacksmith used to be on the lefthand side just before you go into the open market in London Road, I think a butcher's shop is there now. The other market in Upper Gardner Street used to stay open all day on a Saturday; they used to hang lanterns from the canopies over their stalls. There were many bargains to be had, and what with the lanterns, the bustle of the crowd and the surrounding darkness outside, it created a very exciting atmosphere.

As children we played the usual games. I think the most popular was marbles, up and down the gutters which, I hasten to add, were quite clean. Other games seemed to 'take on' at certain times of the year, for example at Easter we had skipping; very thick scaffolding ropes were used and were stretched right across the street. Several of us would all skip together which was all very nice until the rope caught the back of your leg if you missed your step. It would leave a huge weal and was very sore indeed. Whitsun used to see the return of the top and whip, we used to flog them up and down the street like things possessed. Of course the summer holidays saw endless visits to the beach. Living so near the Brighton Railway Station all we had to do was get a tram from there straight down to the seafront for a penny. The sunny days were endless, or so it seemed to us then. The boys of course had their four-wheelers, made from soap boxes and old wheels off of a pram; some were very well made and could reach quite a speed. My two brothers were ten and eleven years older than me so they had different pursuits while I was still very young. My eldest brother played football for the Preston Rovers and often I would take my dolls in their pram, and sit on the grass in Preston Park and watch him play. My other brother used to always be off somewhere on his bike. He and his friends used to go mushrooming; they would set off in the dark and come home in the mornings. Their bicycle lamps were carbide in those days. I remember he used to open the front of the lamp and have to light it, not without difficulty at times, and the smell was dreadful. There are so many memories of my childhood days in Wood Street I will carry them with me with deep fondness forever. I shall always remember the people that lived there, little neat and tidy houses. I am afraid when, after the war and in the name of progress, demolition took place, not only in Wood Street, but other such streets as well, the community spirit, the very heart of Brighton was torn out. It never recovered.

Barbara Coppard

Park Street: off Edward Street (1 Park Street front end papers)

In 1931 I went to live in Park Street and they became the happiest days of my life. It was the families of the street who made life so rich with warmth and happiness. They didn't have much money but you didn't notice that because life was appreciated more than it is today.

My father, Alf Lindsay, was in charge of the Corporation Depot in the street, and our house was inside the depot. Many years ago our house might have been a farm, as in the scullery, as it was known in those days, we had rafters where they hung the carcasses, but my father had all that altered. The town's mortuary was in the depot; Sir Bernard Spilsbury came down to do the postmortems. I remember particularly the trunk crime murder, which kept my dad busy keeping the reporters out. I was a young schoolgirl at the time, and it was a big case as many older people will remember.

Next to our Depot there was a family who used to sell their greengrocery from their horse and cart. We had public baths in Park Street as not many people had bathrooms; they were nice and clean, and I remember Ada who worked there for years. At the bottom of Park Street there was a small Salvation Army Hall. During the last war when my dad had to take his rescue ARP team out, the Major there was always on hand with his team to give drink and food for people who were bombed out. At the bottom across the road was a lovely fish and chip shop where we children used to pop in for a bag of scraps at a penny. We were lucky to have a lovely park at the top of the street. I remember the Braybon family had a house opposite the park and Miss Braybon married Mr Cutress of Forfars.

I remember when they took all the wooden blocks from the old roads up, hundreds of people came into the Depot with their old prams, carts etc. to buy them for their fires. Mind you they had tar on them, but poor people loved them. I think they were fifty for a shilling.

Such happy days of little shops, nice people who owned them and always time to speak to you, shops with character, old fashioned maybe, but lovely, and people seemed more content.

Lastly, I remember as a schoolgirl my parents had a club in the house every Thursday night. It would be darts, cards, crib, billiards (we had a half-size table) and shove ha'penny. We had a piano and mum used to do a big spread of food etc. and I was sent to bed early. I remember playing with a top, a whip, a diabolo and a hoop. We played in the street a lot as there wasn't so much traffic around. I worked for a firm for forty five years, and was in the WAAF in-between. I went back to Clarks Bread Company and I worked in Gigins before Clarks took over. My mother, who is now ninety three years old, remembers all I have written.

But there was always friendship, loyalty and laughter, even tears, in those days everyone helping each other.

Ruby Lindsay

Chapel Street

I was born in June 1932 in Chapel Street. My parents were Fred and Poppy Bowers who lived in number 15. My grandparents (my father's parents) lived next door. I left in 1953 when I married, but my mother and father lived there until they were given a council flat in Whitehawk Road, to make way for a block of flats.

I remember T W Barnes, rag and bone merchants. My mother used to clean their offices during the evening, and I used to help her on Saturday afternoons, when she had a real clean and polish. My father rented our house from them, my aunt and my father both worked for them, also my father's father.

Then came a row of houses, and we lived in one of them. After that there was a yard which we children called 'the jar hole', in those days they bought empty jars, which belonged to Barnes; then there was another row of houses and an alley which led into the High Street. Just above were some garages which lay back from the road; at the top Jordan, a general store, where I got all my sweets. Opposite stood Burroughs, another general store. I clearly remember the old bacon slicer, and they used to sell bags of broken biscuits, which I and my brothers bought on our way to school. Coming back on that side, there was some sort of sawmill; then another row of houses, then Richardson's, yet another rag and bone merchant. I used to call the man there 'Uncle Bill'; he was very good to us kiddies with the odd copper. After that came a row of garages, I think two or three of them belonged to the residents of the next street, Devonshire Place; then a lock up garage, which was used to sort the rags from Barnes; and Simmonds the Brewery, which took up the rest of the street to the pub. We loved that place as kids, as we used it to play all sorts of games, if the boss was not about.

We all used Edward Street a lot as it was our way to school; we all went to Park Street Infants' School, followed by the junior school, St Mary's. I remember a furniture shop called Arnold's on the corner of Devonshire Street; my mother bought all her furniture there. We had a set of dining chairs, two and sixpence each, and we only threw the last of them out when my mother died a few years ago, so you got your money's worth there. I was sent there every Friday as my father was paid with a card and some silver. So I suppose that was the same as buying hire purchase today.

It was a poor street, but a happy street. I clearly remember all the women could be seen whitening their door steps and polishing their door knockers every morning, like clockwork; even if they were ill they still cleaned. I suppose you had to be seen, or you had to hear the local piece of scandal.

During the war we had one of those rotten Anderson shelters in my mother's front room. We kids went to bed in it at night, and all thought it great fun; we were not really aware of the danger from bombs. My father was in the Home Guard, he used to have to go out and sit on the brewery roof for most of the night. I just thought he was very brave to go up to such heights as the brewery roof. My grandmother would not have a shelter as she felt it much safer to take a chair and go under the stairs with her candle, she did that if there was a storm too.

June Drake

Chapel Street: (between 45 St James Street & Edward Street) looking north

Bedford Buildings

I lived in Bedford Buildings for the first eighteen years of my life. We moved out in 1932 and our house was demolished. It had been a happy little house and we had a very pretty garden; we often had people walk by to admire the gardens. Large blocks of flats have been built on the site since.

They were very nice little double-fronted, country-style, large cottages; two up, two down. There were only nineteen houses in the street: eight on the north side, plus the stable yard that had belonged to the Stag Inn when it was a coach house, and eleven on the south side. They were spaced well apart; one side facing to the pavement, the other side each facing the other with gardens between. The toilet was at the far end of the small backyard. When it was dark we took a candle, and if it rained the rain put the candle out. My mother used to red ochre the long front path from gate to door every other day, and we had very pretty window boxes, as well as a lovely garden.

Some of the other families kept chickens or rabbits, and one little old lady had a tortoise that was an attraction; not many about in those days. The yard next to the Stag Inn had a cottage inside the gates; here lived a costermonger lady. She took out her horse and cart loaded with fruit and vegetables each day, summer and winter; dressed in a long black skirt, large sack apron, and a cap, which sat on top of her head of tight golden curls; she was quite a character.

At the top of the street, the Montague Place end, was yet another stable yard, with horses and carriages that plied for hire between the two piers. Later, that was taken over by the 'Boro' bill-posting company. It was a narrow paved street, no road way, so we had no through traffic; therefore it was very quiet and private, and children could play safely. But the milkman and coalman, baker etc. had to work extra hard, as they had to leave their carts at the main road and carry their goods to the door. I well remember our coalman coming up and down the street (we lived right in the middle) with several bags of coal, but he was always cheerful. Of course this type of street also had drawbacks, for a funeral or wedding the whole procession had to walk to the carriages, cars etc. up to the main road. I remember this quite well, as I was ten when my father died, and it seemed such a long way to walk sorrowing.

On Saturday the children all collected rubbish from the shops (cardboard etc...) for mothers to burn in the brick coppers on Monday washday. We only had a few minutes to get to school, as we were surrounded by schools, all the following being within five minutes walk or less: All Souls; St Mary's; Park Street; St John the Baptist. We were also well-catered for with churches and public houses; sadly all the schools and churches have gone except Park Street and St Mary's Church. All Souls School was very popular at that time, but it had only a tiny playground, used for the girls. The boys played in the road in Warwick Street, with a teacher watching for traffic, though there was very little about then.

L O Tincknell

19 Bedford Buildings: (between 3 Montague Place & Upper Bedford Street)

High Street

We lived in number 62 High Street. It was really scruffy, an awful old place with gas lighting. My mother was terrified that we would break the gas mantles when we lit the lamps, because they were expensive. I can remember that we were very poor. We had a flat at the bottom which was terrible; the landlord didn't keep it up at all. My grandmother lived next door in a nice house. She had a big boarding house, because she needed the money, and lots of interesting and foreign people who performed at the Hippodrome in Brighton stayed with her. Her own family used to sleep right up at the top of the house. Although she had no inside toilet, people loved coming to stay; she made them welcome and cooked lovely food. She didn't have a bathroom, so she used to have jugs and basins for washing. There was no bathroom in our house in High Street; I can remember having a tin bath, and going to Park Street Baths once a week. We had a big black range in the basement, which at one time caught on fire, and was absolutely red hot and glowing. My grandfather was a night watchman; he had only one arm.

I can remember war being declared; it was a lovely sunny day and everyone was very serious. I can remember sleeping in an air raid shelter, which they built opposite when those houses were demolished. My brother and I both caught scabies from sleeping there. We had to go to the Sussex County Hospital to be scrubbed. I can remember having to come out of Mount Street School during the war in an air raid warning, and walk down St Mary's Place to a brewery at the bottom for protection. It seems strange now having to walk outside during an air raid to the shelter! We went right down underneath this stone thing under the brewery, which was horrible. There was a water tank also by the air raid shelter, which was meant to be used if a building caught fire, and I can remember a dead cat floating in it. I used to have to queue for potatoes during the war at a greengrocer's on the corner of Blaker Street, and I went and got bags of coal in Poore's in Edward Street with my doll's pram. When we lived at number 58 during the War we had some Czechoslovakian refugees staying with us. A few houses up the road were a family who had ten children. I can remember during the war they couldn't afford to buy their oranges, which were rationed. My mother only had a few coupons, so directly she heard oranges were in the shops she used to tell me to run up the road quickly and get their coupons. She would pay for the oranges and we would share them. You see, they were even poorer than we were. I loved going in their house because there were all these children, and you could run wild and do what you liked.

These houses opposite were demolished either before the war, or at the beginning of the war; nothing to do with the 1950's housing demolition. For a long time it was just ruins, because my brother and I used to say to my mother, 'We're just going to play on the ruins', and she would go crazy because we were going to play on this rubble and get filthy. Even before these houses were demolished I can remember going into a shop; it was a strange, dirty, little, old shop, very dark, and the shopkeeper was a funny little lady. You went in there for a halfpenny worth of sweets in a newspaper cornet. Children used to steal sweets in there because it was so dark, and she couldn't see what you were doing.

High Street: courtyard and passage at rear of 51 High Street

We lived at number 62 for a while, at the beginning of the war, and then moved to number 58 where we had a whole house. Number 58 was much better but it leaked, it was something to do with the type of drainage; when it rained hard or snowed it overflowed and it all came into the house. Mellor and Mellor in St James's Street was our landlord, and the landlord of some of the other houses, and they acted as agents to the owners. We had a big house with a basement, and a floor on the level with the garden, and then two more floors. We didn't use all of the house as there was only my mother, father, my brother and me. We had a beautiful lilac tree in the garden, and every spring it was full of lilac, and all the people around used to have bunches of lilac from us. I can remember having mumps and sitting in the garden under that lilac tree with a swollen face.

During the war we had a reinforced basement, to protect us if the house fell down. My mother would be under this basement with my small brother and me (my father was a fire watcher). Every time the sirens went I always wanted to go to the toilet because I was so scared. The toilet, with a wooden seat, was at the bottom of the garden and I can remember running there and looking up and seeing search lights and being absolutely terrified. There is a pub on the corner of High Street now, which has been there for as long as I can remember. There were also some redbrick houses, which I think are still there, which we thought were posh houses, and we used to say, 'The posh people live over there'. We used to go to the Sunday School every Sunday afternoon; it belonged to St James's Church (which isn't there anymore) in St James' Street. We had to go, there were no ifs or buts about it.

I went to Park Street Infants School, then Mount Street Middle School off Edward Street, and then for a short while to Park Street Seniors until 1945, when my mother died. Then we went to Southend to live with my grandmother, but came back when I was sixteen (1947-8) and lived with my father and stepmother until I was eighteen. I went back to live in High Street again at the top of my father's house in 1954 when I was married. We just had a couple of rooms at the top of the house and I had two children and was expecting another one. I used to have to go down three flights of stairs to cook the meals as the cooker was right down in the basement; by then they were talking of demolishing the houses. When I was about to have my third child (I had three children in three years), we moved to a house in Manor Farm. I couldn't wait to move out of High Street; it was awful when the rain poured in, bits of ceiling falling down, lots of mice, it was really old. My father didn't want to move. He said to my stepmother, 'I'm not going to live in a box'. This house seemed awful to me, but he had so many memories there, and he'd lived there with my mother, and then with my stepmother. He is all right where he is now, but at first he was very much against it. They got a council flat at Craven Vale and are still there.

I was happy living in High Street, the neighbours were very nice. The lady next door to us always made us apple pies as I think she thought we were hungry. Further down the road was a family with two sons, who used to knit us bed socks. The atmosphere there was nice; neighbourly without having people in and out all the time; people were very friendly. Apart from the war it was quite a happy life.

Not all the houses had gardens, some had yards, and a couple of the next door houses had a garden. My grandmother had a sort of yard, with hanging baskets and Dutch clogs with flowers in them. They were small gardens with a huge brick wall at the back, which was the back of Barnes, a rag and bone place at the bottom of Chapel Street, the next street. You got all the awful smells from there because they collected wastepaper, rabbit skins, jam jars etc... I can remember my grandmother skinning rabbits, and standing there waiting for her to do it, because you got about a penny in Barnes for the skin. You got money for jam jars as well, and you asked your Mum to scrape the jam out of them so you could sell the jar for some money for sweets.

There were lots of little businesses. A printing business on our side of the road; there was a sort of slope down to a basement with a platform, and we used to play jumping. It was really dangerous; we used to say, 'Come on, lets go and play up the printer's. I remember a garage a few houses up, where Max Miller, in a very loud suit, took his car to be repaired. At the top of High Street was a little alleyway, which went through to Chapel Street with a couple of little houses up there. At the bottom was an alleyway to the doctor's surgery and some little businesses. We used to cut through the alley on the way to school, but on the way home, if it was dark you used to run because it was a bit scary. At the top of the street were a couple of nice houses with gardens. My aunt lived at number 62 with my grandmother, and left there in the war to marry a soldier. Gordon Hall was a sort of church place which I think they've made into flats now. You tend to remember the more eccentric people, there was a cat's meat lady up the little alleyway, who used to cook and sell meat, and I think had lots of cats as well. It was pretty there; you went up the alleyway and it opened out into about three or four little houses with pretty little gardens. This was a different alley from the one at the top to Edward Street; it was just a small alley which opened into these few houses. There were three alleyways, one at the bottom to the doctor, the one to the cat's meat lady, and then one at the top of High Street which led to another street, and with houses on each side. In Chapel Street there were lots of little Coronation Street type houses next to each other.

That was pretty; you went up the alleyway and it opened out into what must have been about three or four little houses with very pretty little gardens. There was a little grocer's on the corner of Chapel Street called Jordan's, which was a funny little shop (it was there until quite recently) where you could get everything. We bought most of our food from St James's Street and these little shops.

I can remember them coming around on the bikes lighting the lamps, and putting them out when I first lived there.

On public holidays the weather always seemed to be so much better, but I don't know if that is just my imagination. What we used to do was to go down to Pool Valley and get on a bus, and go out to the country to Barcombe Mills and Fulking and Poynings; walking from the Dyke. Lots of walking in the country on Sundays. On Wednesday afternoons, my father's half day, in the winter, we always went to the pictures. In the Regent they had budgerigars all along one side in a wire enclosure. We also had tea and toast on a tray, which must have been really dangerous as we had to pass the trays of tea along rows of people. A man used to come with winkles on a Sunday morning with an organ grinder playing music.

Barbara Wykham

As you walk up from St James's Street, on the left there was a cycle shop on the corner, half in High Street, the other window in St James's Street. I bought my first bike there, a Hercules, for two and sixpence a week, so that I could cycle to work at Fishersgate. Next there was the pub, then a house or two, and a greengrocer, two or three more houses, then Liza's little shop. In Liza's you could buy paraffin, bundles of firewood, bread, even two pennyworth of cheese if you wanted it, little one penny or two penny celluloid dolls with movable arms and legs, sweets, one penny whip, one penny top. We would buy a top and make a whip, all sorts of sweets, and lemonade powder. Also she would swap comics; we would give in two comics for one we hadn't read.

You bought on credit or tick; you were sent for some shopping and told to tell Liza, 'We'll pay at the end of the week'. Her shop window was just a jumble of all sorts of things, and sometimes she wore one orange stocking and one yellow one. The kids taunted her sometimes.

Further up the street was the Sunday School; on feast days we attended St James' Church. When we went to Sunday School we were given a little stamp with a religious picture on it. Tuesday evening, the Girls' Friendly Society held their meetings there. All I ever did was to knit a square. I don't remember ever finishing a square.

Next was a little retail business. I think that's what it was. Next came some nice houses, at least they looked nice on the outside. On the right hand side, from St James's Street there was a garage on the corner, then a fish and chip shop, 2d fish, ld chips - lovely. Then a little lane; I think there was a film developing place down there. As kids we used to go down, peep in the door, and were given empty film spools. Further up High Street there was a wider lane, rather like a small road, and up it, on the right hand corner, was a small cottage on its own. Next the DCL Yeast offices and then houses, one of which was my mum's, and she was always complaining about the smell that came from the back of the house from Barnes Rag and Bone Merchant in Chapel Street. After these half dozen or so houses a motor repair shop. Half way up High Street there was a little house where they sold cat and dog meat, then the Tabernacle, then a couple of shops, then two more shops standing back off the road a bit, then the lane leading to Chapel Street, then about three houses, then Inskip the draper.

In the summer, to get extra pocket money, we would take jam jars, or any rags round to Barnes. I think it was one penny for 2lb jars, half pence for llb; we got one penny a week pocket money. As kids we used to sing under the pier, at the visitors strolling on the pier, hoping they would throw us coins. How we managed to find the coins among the stones I do not know. We used to get strict instructions from mum not to do it, and if we were found out we were reprimanded, or got a good clout. When the races were on at the Race Hill, the horse boxes were unloaded in High Street. I think they must have been getting them ready or just checking them. I've often wondered why they used High Street so far from the Race Hill.

Mum had seven children; but there was another family, just a few doors away with seven children, so in the mornings mum used to say to us, 'Hurry up and get to the bread shop and get any bread left from the day before, before the other family get it', as the day-old bread was cheaper. You were considered posh, in those days, if you had a bathroom in your house, which we didn't have. So when we were small it was a bath in front of the fire in the winter, in the old tin bath, and when we were older we went to the Public Baths in Park Street.

I remember the lamplighter lighting the lampposts in the evening, and the muffin man with his tray on his head, and ringing a bell. Also the fish lady, calling out 'Fresh fish' (but it didn't sound much like the words 'fresh fish'), and the knife sharpening man on his bike, making the sparks fly.

Mavis Cameron

Artillery Street

I lived in a small terraced house in Artillery Street. I felt a little ashamed of the address when we first moved there, as we had lived at 41 Kings Road before. My parents had worked for the owners and we only lived in, but it sounded posher. New owners had taken over the premises in Kings Road and they had a large family so we had to move. My father still worked for them as a House Porter and my mother sometimes cleaned, but we had to find our own accommodation.

My mother was very pleased when she found the house in Artillery Street because it had been newly decorated, but we soon found out that it was 'buggy' and she just kept looking for other places to live from that day on. The house was very small, the front door leading straight into the sitting room, the kitchen at the back and two rooms upstairs. I can't remember a bathroom, so I don't think there was one, and I suppose there was a toilet in the back yard, but I have no memory of it.

Along the top of Artillery Street ran Upper Russell Street, where there was a wholesale greengrocer or butcher; and further along was a lovely Jewish baker where they used to have the most wonderful rolls. On Sunday mornings we used to go along and buy those rolls hot. Just near there was a big newsagent and confectioner, at least it seemed big to me, and opposite on a corner was a baker, Gigins, I think, where we bought the first cut and wrapped loaves called 'Cream of the South'. At 8 Blucher Place there was a very big yard which was shared by three houses, numbers 8, 9 and 10. My friend, who lived at number 8, and I loved singing and dancing, we were always in the shows at our school, Middle Street. We used to go along to Gigins and buy stale cakes, you could get a lot for tuppence. Then, with all the little kids in the street, we used to go to this yard and make a kind of tent out of clothes horses, sheets and things. We sat all the children down and gave them stale cakes and lemonade made with lemonade powder; then my friend Joyce and I used to sing and dance. I was always Alice Faye and I think Joyce was Betty Grable. The kids used to love it. When Joyce's family moved to number 5 the shows had to stop because we lost the fantastic back yard.

I did well at school and passed the scholarship to go to Varndean; in fact I passed the first part for Brighton and Hove High School too. Six of us were put forward for the written exam and I was the only one from my school to pass. Then I had to go for my oral exam, but I didn't pass that. I expect I didn't speak well enough.

My father was proud and pleased that I had passed the scholarship but he couldn't believe it. He was very much 'I know my place' sort of person. He'd been in the Army for years (running away from home at thirteen and lying about his name and age). He was a batman to an officer and he felt very lowly. Every Christmas his old officer would send him 10 shillings in a card, of course to the name he had used in the army not to his real name. He couldn't believe that his daughter had passed this exam. My mother was a country girl, brought up in Waterhall, Patcham. She seemed quite pleased but I don't think she would have minded either way.

We received a grant of £10 a year to cover expenses, which didn't cover everything, but I was just happy that I was able to go. Joyce didn't pass for Varndean but passed for the Intermediate School in York Place. I loved Varndean during the first year and didn't mind attending without a good friend. I had always been very outgoing and soon made friends at the school. I was in the top class and studied French and Latin. Unfortunately the war disrupted my education and we had to share the school with

children from a school in London. During this time I began to lose interest; when all my friends started work I began to get restless. My parents had signed to say that I would attend Varndean until I was sixteen, but during the war they weren't so strict and you could leave as long as you had a job. My father got me a job in King's Road, in a jeweller's called South Coast Stone Co., so I was allowed to leave. I don't remember anyone trying to stop me although I was still in the top class. I hated this job as it was only threading beads all day, and I left after two weeks; I then worked for Freeman Hardy & Willis the shoe shop for three years. Then I was directed to the S. S. Brighton in West Street, where we made condensers for radios, but this soon finished as we couldn't get the parts. I then had a choice of a laundry or the buses. I didn't fancy the buses much, but I didn't like the idea of a laundry, so I went on the buses and loved it. I even thought about going back on the buses after my first husband died, but you had to drive as well and I couldn't do that.

I had a marvellous childhood. Joyce and I attended the Band of Hope at Holy Trinity Church. We didn't know what the Band of Hope was for at the time, but I've learnt since that its something to do with not drinking. We also attended Brownies there and you had to go to Sunday School if you went to Brownies. We didn't particularly want to got to Sunday School although it was lovely if you were the one to carry the flag.

We used to go all over the place on our own from about the age of five, we would spend days on the beach all on our own. We used to play in the fishermen's boats, because I knew nearly everybody there as I had lived in Kings Road. From our old house we could walk from our cellar through the arches to the beach, and my father knew everyone. We would spend ages in the sea.

Everyone was neighbourly in Artillery Street, and children seemed much safer in those days. I remember my childhood with affection and remember the times when we all went to the Hippodrome on Friday night. We always had the same seats up in the Gods and afterwards went to the Gloucester Pub where they had a children's room. Joyce and I would wait for the stars to leave the Hippodrome and get their autographs. We had quite a few including Florrie Ford, The Crazy Gang and Max Miller. We also went to the children's programmes at the Princes Cinema in North Street and the Academy in West Street. On bonfire night they had big bonfires on the beach with fireworks. I can smell that smell now, it was so exciting.

I don't think that we were poor, in fact we were probably better off than many in the area. We always ate well and I had some nice clothes. Some streets in the area seemed poorer; Cannon Street seemed poorer to me as a child, the children seemed more ragged than we were, but perhaps I'm mistaken. Other streets such as Grenville Place and Cannon Place seemed to be more wealthy.

Pat Sprinthall

We lived at number 12 Artillery Street. There was so much to do around Artillery Street, you could go down the bottom of the road and you were on the beach. There was the Palladium around the corner, and the ice rink, there were the shops at the top, in Western Road. Around the clock tower the pie man was a familiar sight, he used to stand on the corner of Aire Street. He had a funny little black oven on a

Artillery Street (now Churchill Square) north east corner looking south east

29

barrow with iron wheels and he would heat the pies up for you; there were also hot chestnuts for sale. There was a lovely fish and chip shop called Bardsley's in Upper Russell Street; we had to have a bag of scraps quite often as we didn't have much money, like everyone who lived along that street. It was quite a noisy street with the brewery, and there was always somebody coming and going, lorries galore too, so we couldn't play in the street. But at weekends it wasn't too bad, everybody was out sitting on the doorsteps having a chat.

We would go down to Black Rock, and do winkle picking and we would come back and my Mum would boil them all up; they were horrible little screaming things. Then we would go out and sell our winkles thrupence for half a pint or sixpence a pint. We did any kind of money-making thing that we could do. We would walk right out to Stanmer Park, pick loads and loads of bluebells and primroses and tie them on a stick and come back up Western Road and sell them like two little waifs. We were always doing something. From the houses that had been bombed we used to collect piles of wood and we would come back home and chop them into nice little bundles, then we would go round and sell these. My Mum was quite pleased with us, because we were busy but earning a few pence; it wasn't a lot but it always helped. They were hard working days for children, but it was fun because you were going out finding things to do, coming back and working to make a few pence.

My Mum had eight children altogether but she lost four of them. The houses were strange in Artillery Street, tall, dim and smelly, all slums. My Mum used to get welfare because my Dad didn't work much. On Mondays it used to be 'Here's your Father's suit, go up the pawnshop'; or 'Take the sheets off the bed, wash them and take them along to uncle's, get a few bob till the end of the week'; which I did quite often. We used to have to go to Royal York Buildings and get meal tickets for dinners, because they didn't give you that much money in those days, and instead gave you tickets for meals, or a pair of shoes or boots. At Christmas we used to get little parcels; my Mum had to go and put her name down on the list to receive this. It was scrimp and scrape, and we were always on the move from one slummy house to another. It wasn't a case of 'phoning up for a removal van, we had to hire a barrow and I used to love piling everything on the barrow and helping to push it through the streets.

A lot of the houses were owned by private landlords and were quite reasonable and cheap, but if they had been taken over by the council they could have probably done something with them. It is a shame really they are not there anymore. Nearly every street I lived in Brighton has gone. Although they were slum areas they were happy areas. You hear lots of people say in those days you could go out and leave your front and back door open, and nobody would go in. If anyone did call in it was to say 'Hello', or 'Can I help you?' or 'I've got the kettle on!' Even though kids had scraps and fights it didn't last or boil into anything with the neighbours. I can't see where all that understanding of the years gone by went.

Our house in Artillery Street had a couple of steps up to the front door; as you went in to the front room there were two funny little cupboards each end, with a cupboard underneath and a fireplace in the middle. Then you went round the passage way to go through to the kitchen and scullery and there was a little funny back yard with a cobbled wall, and the toilet at the end. My brother and I used to try and plant things in the wall, because we'd seen people with plant pots hanging outside, and thought they looked nice; we used to hammer at the wall trying to put these plants in to make them grow! Then downstairs there was the basement which was always dark and dim, but we used to go down there in the winter because it was warmer. There was a fireplace down there and we used to have the light on; gas light then, with gas mantles. Upstairs there was a landing with funny wooden stairs with wobbly banisters; the electricity upstairs did not work and noone ever came and did anything about it. There were two bedrooms on that floor and then upstairs was an attic room which I shared with my sister; it had a pull-up window where we used to look out over the roof. Most of the houses down there were the same, but across the other side of the road at the top end of Artillery Street, they were different; they were laid back and had a little gate and a garden in front. There was about four of them. Further down the road the houses were similar to ours.

Our house smelt damp, musty but warm sometimes. We had bugs and had to be fumigated which left a terrible smell that took ages to go. When we came back all these bugs were lying on the floor; I thought they were ladybirds. I should imagine every house down there had some because the walls were like sponge and hardly any of the electricity worked; quite often you would put the switch on and get a shock. Once our ginger kitten was electrocuted from the bad fitting switches, and killed.

Quite a few men down the street worked at Tamplin's; it was a busy little street. Down the bottom was Russell Street which was quite a busy little thoroughfare because it separated West Street from Artillery Street. There was St Paul's Church which is still there, and the Odeon and the ice rink.

Down the bottom of Russell Street, we used to cross the road and go down a flight of steps to the beach. When the beach was barb-wired during the war, my brother and I were standing at the top; all of a sudden these sirens started, and so we started to run home and I was really scared. The sky seemed to be really black all of a sudden, because the planes were blocking out the sun and the houses were so tall, it was horrible. Quite a few shells dropped just at the top of Artillery Street and round the back in Upper Russell Street where a bomb fell, and we hadn't got home yet. We heard this explosion and just stood there and went in this funny little doorway behind a telegraph pole and we dared not move. After a while we came out; we ran up the road to have a look whose house it was that had been hit.

Another place I remember was the Scratch in Lewes Road, or the Arcadia where the Labour club is now. It was a picture place my Mum used to go to quite often because you could get in there for sixpence or a shilling. It had a long foyer leading up before you got in the cinema and during the war a lot of Mums used to leave their babies in the pushchairs outside in this foyer, whilst they went in to watch the pictures. Sometimes she would take me to the pictures, but I would have to keep going out to see if the kids were all right. She also went to the Palladium on the seafront at the bottom of Russell Street, just around the corner from Artillery Street. If we came home and my Mum wasn't at home, she was in the pictures losing her blues, and I don't blame her, because they didn't have anything for entertainment.

Artillery Street was fun to live in; it's a shame really you lose contact with all those people.

Mrs Goodwin

Churchill Square

Grenville Place

Before the war it was a marvellous letting area, the same visitors would come year after year, and they would go for a swim before breakfast. My father had a business in Grenville Place, fruiterer and greengrocer. He was there from 1918, and when he died in 1950 the business was still there, until the corporation more or less pinched it off me around 1960. That was when they made compulsory purchase orders of all the property along there. Then they built Churchill Square.

When I left school at fourteen I helped in the business with my father. I continued running my father's business after he died, but I did this more or less in the background because I was a Post Office Telephone engineer, supervisor and officer; I ran the books and sorted things out with the business at weekends. My wife helped to run the shop.

I lived above my father's shop until I was married. During the war my wife took a flat in Grenville Place to be near my people, because we lived along the Gladstone Terrace, Lewes Road. They had bombs along there, and of course it worried my people, so she took a flat in Grenville Place and we were there until we had to move out.

It's not the same now. Everybody was neighbourly. Having a business you knew every one, they all knew you and would speak to you, but you don't see a soul now. You may only see your next door neighbour sometimes. It's surprising when you move. I think business makes a great difference, people know you better then. There were all sorts of businesses down there. In Russell Street was a small bootmaker; he lived at number 37 and had a little business on the corner of Russell Street as it bends round. Then on the other side was a small coal merchants by the name of West; it was only a small place, but I think they used to go and get winkles, and they would sell them at sixpence a pint. I remember Milton Place, it was a rather nice area. All the streets were quite small and mainly residential.

We didn't have many children in Grenville Place. There were the two sons next door; my father bought a boat, and they had a boat, and we used to go out on the sea a lot, but I don't remember a lot of playing out in the streets. Our boat was a 14ft rowing boat; we used to go out in the afternoons, go fishing and all sorts of things; lie out in the lovely sunny weather; read, throw the lines over and just rely on what happened while you lay there.

The area was quite busy because of the shops; if we wanted to play we went down to the seafront, there weren't any parks nearby. I was in the choir in Chapel Royal in North Street; I went to the Sunday school first of all, and I was also in the Scout group; the scout hall was the church hall in New Road. We used to go on outings to Hassocks; there used to be a fairground there with mini-roundabouts and bicycles and tricycles.

When I was a teenager I used to go out along the front and on the piers, and to the pictures and dance halls; the Academy, and the Regent on Queens Road. Then there used to be one on the sea front called the Palladium, at the bottom of Russell Street.

Cannon Street : (now Churchill Square) looking south

It was only a tiny little place, but they had good films. The Duke of York's was too far out. There was also one just before Montpelier Road.

We used to go out when my father got a car, and I bought a car when I was 18; a two-seater sports car. Not very many people owned cars; my father and I both had a garage. His car was larger than mine and he paid seven and six to rent his garage, and I paid five shillings. Both were lock-up garages with electric lights! What it would cost you today! The best petrol was one and ninepence a gallon.

During the war, there wasn't a lot to be had in the way of goods; you got what you could, but most afternoons you closed because there just wasn't the stuff to be had. You just got what you could and sold it to your customers; when it was gone that was it. Brighton used to look very different during the war, with all the barbed wire on the beach, but I didn't see much of it. It was pretty empty here during the war. My family didn't have an air-raid shelter in Grenville Place during the war; my father just stayed put.

Inside the house at Grenville Place there was a room, at the back of the shop, which was used as a store room. This was on the ground floor, together with a large kitchen. Then of course, there was a yard and an outhouse with an outside toilet. Then on the first floor there was a bathroom, which was a room converted by my father before the war; a bedroom; and a front sitting room. Up on the next floor were the two bedrooms. My mother had a copper at first, and then my father brought her a twin-tub. There was a large kitchen range, as the kitchen was very large, but this was hardly used. So my father took it out, leaving the copper at the back, but I don't remember my mother doing any washing in it. There was just the three of us living there, I didn't have any brothers or sisters. It was a big place, most of the properties around that area were very similar. We had electricity, with a gramophone, a radio and a television from around 1950.

The people in the area had a strong community spirit, they would always come and help you, and they'd do anything for you, very helpful all round. Quite a convivial neighbourhood. Everyone knew everyone, and they would all come into the shop and talk; not like in the supermarkets today where they just take your money and slap your goods down, nobody knows anyone in there.

The managers of most of the shops, and one or two of the owners of shops in Western Road, lived over the properties that were on that side. There was, however, no difference in status between the people who lived here; they all mixed well. They all used to come in the shop and talk about different things, how business was etc. It was really quite a good area to be in because it was central, you had everything around you.

People did tend to shop in their local corner store. There weren't so many of the big stores like today, they were all smaller shops. Everywhere was very well kept. The women would be sweeping their fronts in the morning, and my father always used to get a boy to wash the windows, and the front of the shop would be washed down, together with the pavement and everything. It was a very clean area. All the shops down Western Road all looked clean and bright.

It will never be the same in Brighton again. You'll never get the visitors like you used to. Down Queen's Road you couldn't walk for the people who were flocking down from the station, not only at weekends, but in the daytime as well; and getting in the cinemas was virtually impossible. It was really a booming place in those days. The Hippodrome had the most marvellous shows and acts. My father and mother and me used to go every week. They had magical acts, and lions and tigers. All the old-timers and London artists used to come down, from the 1920's until just before the war. Brighton was at its height from after 1926, in the thirties, until the war years. And that's why it was always busy down our way, as people came from the station to find lodgings in Grenville Place and the surrounding areas. And the hotels, which weren't the huge places that they are today, were always busy. The beach was crowded, you had a job to find a space. In my early youth there was Jack Shepherd's, along by Volk's Railway opposite Madeira Drive, and that was like a pierrot show on the beach and there was another one on the other side of the Palace Pier, which crowds of people would watch. And there were the bands on the bandstand at the bottom of West Street at one time, and one on the way to Hove Lawns. I think they were the most prosperous years for Brighton, leading up to the war years, really a boom town then, but now it is more or less a business area, more offices than boarding houses.

There is nothing to attract people any more. The beaches used to be lovely and clean, and you had fishing boats down there and fair sized pleasure boats which would hold fourteen people. There was the Skylark, and a man named Scott. Everybody used to just leave their boats on the beach, you would just have to put a couple of struts underneath it and it would be quite safe. There was a man near us called Scott who had a large motor boat and he would fill it up and take people out for a ride on the sea, a terrific amount of business they had. 'Anymore for the Skylark!', they used to call out.

There used to be a fish market down on the seafront, just a little way along from the Palace Pier coming west. The boats would bring their fish in, and you would buy it all fresh off the barrows. Then they moved the market out to where the fruit market was. Some people used to go out all night, come in with fish at six in the morning, and start selling it right away.

My father initially rented the shop from Magnus Volk, the railway owner, who owned a lot of property in Brighton. Then it came up for auction and my father bought it. When the corporation wanted it they just paid a pittance for it. I believe that the thought of having to move away killed my mother, the thought of leaving the place after living there for over forty years preyed on her mind. She was alive when the notice was served but died before we left, she was taken ill suddenly. I think that when you have lived in a place for that amount of time you feel very strongly about leaving. I went to see the councillors about the business and said that it had been in my family forty years and at the present time it was my mother's livelihood. I said you can see the state of the property, it was in a beautiful condition, my father had spent money on it and had it well looked after. They said they were not interested in the business or the property, but were only interested in, and only paying for, the ground that it stood on. I didn't get enough to buy this place, I had to borrow money. They only gave six months' warning for me to find somewhere else, but of course it's different now. They can't do it now, they would have to pay for the value of the property and everything. Today with a business of good standing, I would have got a good figure for it.

It was one of those unfortunate things that there was a compulsory purchase order. It wasn't much good complaining against the council. When a compulsory purchase order was put on my house, the council didn't offer me any new accommodation, and as they were only prepared to pay for the land. I had to borrow to buy my new house. Most of the other people in the street also owned their properties and faced a similar plight.

Then we moved; I haven't seen a soul from there since I left. I didn't go and see the area when it was pulled down because I didn't really want to see it demolished. It'll never be the same again.

John Whitwell

Upper Russell Street

My family moved to 11 Upper Russell Street in 1919. My brothers Vic and Ken were born at this house in 1921 and 1922. I was given the same name as my father who had bought a horse and cart in order to sell vegetables when he came out of the army. He then took a lock-up shop facing down Artillery Street, and became a greengrocer for a number of years.

Our house at 11 Upper Russell Street had been built between 1815 and 1830. The basement had railings in front of it and colonnaded arches. It was in a group of five houses which had been very well built. There was no water in the kitchen at all but there was an outhouse where there was a shallow sink, and a toilet in the back garden. For hot water we would boil a kettle on the range in order to wash each morning, and we bathed in a tin bath in front of the fire. There was also a dining area in the basement. Upstairs on the ground floor we had two rooms at the front, one was used as a bedroom and one as a kind of lounge. On the top floor there were two more bedrooms. The house was considered to be very nice, with big rooms, and although my parents only rented it, my father must have been doing quite well in order to live there. I can't remember what the rent was but I know that it was collected. We also paid rent for the shop. Our house was lit by gas to start with, but the shop had paraffin flood lamps only.

When I was old enough I went to St. Margaret's Church, which was by Regency Square, off Cannon Place. I used to go in the morning as a choir boy, to Sunday School in the afternoon, and again in the evening as a choir boy; three times every Sunday. My brothers did the same when they were old enough. The Church of St. Margaret's was very beautiful and it had balconies all the way round where you could sit. My mother was quite religious but my father wasn't. All the children went to a Sunday School then and they always had 'best' clothes to wear even if they were poor. The area around Cannon Street was full of public houses. They were the sort with sawdust on the floor so were meant for working men; you didn't get many women sitting in them. In Artillery Street there was a public house at the top, which was run by the brothers Vine, and called the Artillery Arms. When you went down Russell Street there was a pub half way down, which also had a gymnasium for boxers to train in. I saw Tommy Farr and Jack Pettifer, as well as most of the well known boxers of that time training there. In that small area there must have been at least twelve pubs. There was drunkenness as the pubs opened long hours.

In Russell Street, opposite the brewery, virtually next door to it, there was another church which many people don't know about, called the Church of the Resurrection. This church was built, I understand, because St. Paul's was full of the gentry and the wealthy. Wagner decided to build this church for the poor and the children of the area. He had designed St. Bartholomew's and wanted another large church; the brewery objected to the height. Instead of building the church up he built it 30 ft down. I went into it when I was young and you had to go down steps to the nave. It got so damp and bad that they decided to close it down and in later years I remember it being used as a meat store and later still by Tamplin's Brewery to store their beer barrels. I understand that it was a very good store because it was so damp and cool.

I spent the best years of my life around the Russell Street area, the spirit was so friendly and if you were in trouble people would help you. Most people stayed in the area and there wasn't much movement in or out, so we knew everyone. Our front door was never locked, not even at night, and there was very little theft. You never saw litter or paper in the streets like you do now, and although there was poverty around everything was clean. As I walked to school past those little two up, two down cottages in Russell Place the women used to be out stoning their steps with hearth stone; they did this everyday and the steps always looked spotless. Although some children went around with patches in their trousers and poor shoes, they were not anywhere near as poor as the people from Carlton Hill, where we considered the really poor people lived.

One of my jobs was to help my mother on washday, Monday. She would heat the water in a copper and I had to turn the wringer to wring out the clothes before hanging them up to dry.

As I got older I used to help my father with the greengrocer's shop. In those days we used to go down to Bartholomews to get vegetables at 4am in the morning. We would push a wheelbarrow, down Artillery Street and along the seafront, to Bartholomew's, to collect the greengroceries and bits and pieces, and push it all the way back along the seafront and back up to our shop. Potatoes and bananas were delivered by van in bulk. My father used to have a store in Cannon Mews, which in the early days had been stables for the horses of the gentry of the area. When times were good my father opened another shop just down from the twitten leading from Russell Square, and my mother helped out with the business. While his business was thriving my father provided the greengroceries to the Grand Hotel, as the back entrance was in Cannon Street. He had a motorbike and sidecar and later a car, and would go to Brighton Races in a horse and carriage with his pals, when things were good.

As time went by my father had to get out of his shop, because the owners wanted to convert it back to a house, so he took a place opposite, at the top of Artillery Street on the left. It was a large garage place that he had for a few years, but I can't remember how long. After that, things started going a bit bad with business. I don't really know why, but I think the bigger stores took the customers, and he had to give up the store in the mews and things deteriorated. Then, between the late 30's and 1939, we moved house to the bottom of Artillery Street, into what was an empty pub converted back to a house, and he gave up the greengrocery business. He then went to work for Tamplins, who had taken over from Kidd & Hotblack Ltd, which took up two thirds of one side of Artillery Street. My father was a small man, but he was very strong and he could carry a sack of potatoes under one arm.

The area was considered classy in the 1920's because we had Cannon Place, Russell Square and Regency Square. In Russell Square there was Moore's Garage, and you could walk through there to Preston Street, and see all the Rolls Royces as you went. The green areas in front of these Squares were for the residents only, and the gates would be locked. Children had nowhere to play, so we spent most of our time on the beach watching the herring catches. My father had relations who were fishermen, and I used to get herrings from my uncle Joe Harman, if I was on the beach when he came in. The streets were very mixed, and many of the small houses contained hotel workers and fishermen.

Cannon Street, apart from the pub, was mainly residential, except for the top corner, where there was a furniture shop and a baker. Then you had Artillery Street with a pub and my father's shop at the top, and houses all the way down on the right, until you reached the pub where we would later live. On the left, the brewery dominated the road and extended into Russell Street. It took up the majority of the street, and originally stabled horses on site. Later, when Tamplins took over, they had lorries, and it became very noisy in the mornings as most of them drove up Artillery Street and into the Western Road area. Western Road wasn't widened then and it was very busy with traffic on such a narrow road. Artillery Street was quite wide, I would say about 25 foot between pavements, but other streets were smaller and could just allow two cars to pass.

At the bottom of Russell Street was the Alhambra Variety Hall, where I saw the Crazy Gang; it then became the Palladium Opera House where we went to the cinema for 6d. There was a dairy where I would go to get a jug of milk each morning, as well as butter taken from a large pat. If you bought milk from the street they would ladle it out into your own container. We also had the onion men, the muffin man with his bell, the winkle man, fresh herrings and watercress sold in the streets.

Recently I paced my steps along where Upper Russell Street used to be, and I think my house was just where the entrance to the car park is now. Some of the houses that went were lovely; those in Grenville Place for instance were considered to be very attractive; and those in Russell Place, although only small, would be very attractive today.

George William Harman

My father ran Fellingham's Electrical Contractors at 116 North Street, just above Queen's Square. He sold electrical appliances in the shop, but he installed and maintained the electricity of many schools in Brighton; hotels; Vokins; Soper's; and country houses. We lived above the shop when I was young, and I would frequently walk around the area looking at the shops.

I had a friend who lived in Artillery Street, behind Western Road where Churchill Square now stands. She lived in one of two cottage houses at the top of the Street, with a tall fence in front of them. It had a long garden, with a stony path leading to the front door, and a large tree in the garden. I don't know why this house was different from the others. I also had an aunt who lived in Cannon Street. Her house had three storeys and spiky railings in front of it. There were some better houses in Cannon Place, and I went to some lovely parties in one of them. Grenville Place also had some attractive houses.

Joyce Fellingham

Elder Street

42 Elder Street was a three storey house with a basement, over which was a grating; we used to look up from this to see the weather and watch people walking over it. The house was cool in summer, cosy without the need of central heating in winter.

The Railway Viaduct across Argyle Road could be seen as we played in the street, we often watched the steam trains go over it. From the top front bedroom we could see the railway workshops and paint shed, where they repaired and painted the old steam engines. From the back top window, you could see the fish and chips being prepared in the rear of 'Bostock', the fish shop. At the other end of the street (York Hill) was a blind merchants, called 'Wilmhurst', where they made all types of blind; and a little general store called 'Baldock' just round the corner; in York Hill itself was a paper and sweet shop called 'Croydon'. There was a Public House on the corner (New England Road end) called the 'Old Hoss' two doors from us; I think it was originally called the 'Old Horse'. Between the gap of the fish and chip shop and the butchers, we could see Preston Circus fire station and hear the big brass bell clang when the fire engines went out. At one place about half way along the street, on the top side, there was a very small general shop, selling anything from a gallon of paraffin to a half penny Oxo cube; further along an old Public House was converted to a house, by the side of which was a gate cum door. Children, myself included, slipped through to Elder Row if we wanted to dodge someone. On the upper corner, New England Road end, we had a tiny barber's shop, a watch and clock maker's shop; some of these people were also part-time firemen.

I lived at 42 Elder Street from the age of five years, my sister was born there. The house itself was owned originally by 'Bushby' the plumbing firm. It was one of the two houses in the street to have hot water and a bath, the water heated by a geyser over the bath, with a big brick copper for wash day, under which was a fire to heat the water. The bath itself was in the kitchen, with a top which doubled as a table to eat from, or a bench for cooking. For keeping the food cool there was a larder on a shelf in the basement backyard of most houses, with a small roof.

They were happy days, although some of the time our father was out of work, but we seemed to manage. Mother went out to work as a domestic servant part-time; to help out I had a Saturday job. The thing that I appreciated was the communication with the neighbours, no one felt isolated and left out of anything going on around us.

Betty Russell

I lived at number 25 Elder Street from 1930 until 1957 or '58. Our house was three storeys high with a backyard where we bred rabbits. I lived there with my two brothers and my Mum and Dad and later my husband. We had six rooms altogether. For lighting we used candles or gas. On the bottom floor was the kitchen or scullery with a copper for heating up water. We had a range which was leaded. There were three bedrooms and a front room. Mondays were always washday. Elder Row was a tiny street and Elder Place was similar to Elder Street.

The shops were open long hours and if you wanted anything you just knocked and they would let you in. We shopped at the open market and at the local grocer's shop where we got things on tick if we were short of money.

I remember the Doodle Bugs during the war, because one passed Elder Street and hit the Viaduct. I had just come home from school and was told to go to the shops, but I didn't, and was lucky I had a near escape, because I missed the bomb falling! During the war I remember a breeze block coming through the window of the boys' room and it missed them.

We played street games and went to the park. We used to buy a pennyworth of stale cakes (yesterday's batch) from Gigins the baker opposite the Duke of York's. Mum made us some lemonade and we used to stay in the park all day. There used to be swings on the Level, and a pond. We used to play gingerbread knockers, hop-scotch, and with a whip and spinning top. At Easter there used to be two teams on the Level from the public houses who used to use a scaffolding rope for skipping. We used to make Easter bonnets and wear patent leather shoes. I remember going blackberry and flower picking at Waterhall, Patcham; and picking primroses and cowslips at Ditchling Beacon. I was in the Girls' Friendly Society which was similar to the Guides. There were lots of entertainment as children and we used to play dominoes with our grandparents, which the television spoiled.

We had a good relationship with the police, if they thought you were misbehaving they would give you a quick clip around the earhole. If you were naughty there was no harm done, you would just get a rap on the knuckles, the same as at school. We knew the local bobby and if you were in trouble you could go to him.

My father was a platelayer on the railways. My Dad's job on the railways meant we got privilege tickets for the immediate family, which were reduced, and free tickets on the trains; we were lucky to go, others couldn't afford travel.

If a neighbour fell ill we would still help, despite having fallen out before. Neighbours were neighbours then, and you would share everything that you got. We had street parties and everyone knew everyone else. The older people who lived in the old houses were scattered everywhere after Elder Street was demolished and they had no contact with each other, and didn't like the new houses they were moved to.

Mrs Barnett

When my grandparents were married they lived in Belton Road Brighton, but due to the distance and the unsocial hours grandfather worked, they moved to Elder Street, which was a mere ten minute walk from the Old West Signal Box, close to New England Road. I was just six months old in 1936 when my parents moved into 33 Elder Street, to run the household following the death of my maternal grandmother. So I spent my childhood and formative years in this little community around Preston Circus. Apart from my service in the Navy I lived in this house until I married in 1948.

The household consisted of my grandfather, a retired signalman with the Southern Railway for fifty years (it was his job that prompted him to move to this house as it was close to his work); my second cousin who had been orphaned in 1916, and virtually adopted by my grandparents; and finally there was 'the lodger', a regular fire-man attached to the fire station at Preston Circus.

My father, who was born in the house in 1895, had almost finished his apprentice-ship as a plumber with Frank Bushby of New England Road, when he was

Elder Street: (near Preston Circus) looking north

mobilised into the Army at the outbreak of the First World War in 1914. He returned to civilian life in 1921 and married mother in 1923. He had various jobs such as driving a horse and cart, but as a child I always knew him as a builder's labourer, with frequent periods of unemployment, until he was again called to the colours in September 1939.

By the mid 1930's my cousin Ed and the fireman had left home, and although Dad was in and out of work, and money was in short supply, we were always well fed, well clothed and warm; but on reflection Mum must have had quite a struggle to balance the budget.

The house itself was the standard two up, two down. It had a basement living room, with daylight emanating from a grating in the pavement above the 'area', kept whitewashed to reflect the maximum light. All the cooking was done in the back scullery, a cold room which looked out on the backyard and had the only water supply, a cold water tap over a red earthenware sink. Of course it had the 'copper', that cauldron which was stoked up every Monday for the weekly wash.

The cooking was done on a rather ancient, black iron, gas cooker; but by far the biggest item in the scullery was the mangle, which was, I remember, rather partial to little fingers if they wandered too close to the rollers. Naturally the WC was across the backyard; it was cold, damp and very dark.

Only the kitchen, scullery and 'front room' had gas lights; candles were used elsewhere. In the late '40's Dad installed a bath and water heaters, while a friend and I wired the house for electricity. The house was rented; the original landlords are unknown to me. However I do recall being taken as a child to the Pavilion Buildings in Brighton to 'pay the rent', presumably to an agent.

To a child none of this was relevant, I was happy and well-loved. Christmas was magical and it never seemed to rain. I think one of my earliest recollections was connected with the 'lodger' ... all firemen lived around the fire station, and their houses were connected by wire to the control room, so that when the bells rang in Headquarters their houses also were alerted. Even the lights in the Duke of York's cinema next to the fire station were dimmed to recall the firemen. This alarm was my cue to run around to the 'Circus' to watch those big red monsters emerge from the fire station (much smaller than the present one), with their bells clanging and the firemen donning their helmets.

At the end of the street we had a pub, 'The Old Hoss'; a barber; Mr Francis the chimney sweep; and among others Mr Bushby, who had the plumber's shop, and who, incidentally, re-employed my father when he was demobbed in 1945. It is interesting to note that the business, under the direction of Mr Bushby's son, has recently closed down. By far the most memorable shop was the one where everything from petit beurre biscuits to paraffin was sold. I used to be fascinated when the shopkeeper converted a little square of newspaper into a cone and filled it with sweets.

The world was just around the corner in London Road; those shops were like magnets to me: Bradshaw, full of bikes and dinky toys; Hobbies, where you could buy real steam locomotives; and of course Sainsbury's, with baskets full of eggs fronting the shop on the pavement.

The sound that still rings in my rather mature ears is that of the shunting engines of the Southern Railway. They would haul the laden goods' wagons up the incline backing onto Boston Street and then, after uncoupling them, would shunt these wagons into the sidings with a very loud 'bing-bang-bong' noise that reverberated all down the line.

Of course the war was to be the turning point for us all, life was never the same again; some of the men did not return from active service. The street itself was damaged by a bomb that fell in Elder Place during a daylight raid.

However, with peace, normality began to return, and in spite of talk of rehousing and slum clearance, which must have been instigated some twenty years earlier, my parents remained in the house until the late 50s, just before the street was demolished.

Harry Mitchell

I was working on the railway when we lived in Elder Street after the last war. We lived there for 18 months, in a three storey house with a back basement. We couldn't live downstairs because the rats had taken it over. The whole area was full of rats. They used to come from the stables along Elder Street, where all the horses were kept for general carting and transport. We stayed out of that basement, the rats had it to themselves. I was glad to get out of that place, I can tell you. There was a men's club in Elder Street, 'The Bartholemew Men's Club. I used to help them get the club ready after I had my accident on the railway. Popular place it was.

Albert Wheatley

I moved to Elder Street in 1943 or '44. The house was small: two bedrooms and a slip room, front room for special occasions, kitchen with a coal range, scullery, no bathroom, we washed and bathed in the scullery; the coal was kept under the back stairs. Everyone in the area lived in the same way. Some people brought up seven children in these houses. Our rent was under ten shillings a week, but I never knew who the owner of the house was as we paid the rent to an agent. Repairs were hardly ever carried out, there seemed no point as the houses were due to come under the bulldozer. As the condition of the houses became worse, some bug infested, I don't think that many people shed tears about leaving when the time came. It was a happy community, we all helped each other. A group of nuns called 'The Little Sisters of Bethany', who were attached to St Bartholomew's Church, made regular visits to anyone in trouble, financial or otherwise.

I worked at the railway as a carriage cleaner during the war, while Mum gave me a hand with the children. Most of the men in the street worked on the railway, though they were away during the war.

Beatrice Kessler, who died shortly after this interview.

Richmond Buildings

My father, Harry Croydon, opened a newsagents shop in Richmond Buildings in 1912, and he stayed there until Richmond Buildings and the area round it were condemned in 1958. Some of the people in the street during that period were: Harry Sinden, undertaker; a greengrocer; fish and chip shop; cat and dog's meat shop; wholesale clothing; barber; secondhand shop; haberdasher; grocer; another secondhand shop; another fish and chip shop; boot repairer; gas fitter; watercress seller; herbalist; Mrs Wragg, secondhand clothes; sweet shop; Gates, timber merchants; Lennox Arms Pub; greengrocer; another greengrocer; another boot repairer; retail clothing; tailor; butcher; tin smith; another boot repairer; hairdresser; another boot repairer; another sweet shop; Dr John Vance's surgery; John Marshall, chimney sweep; St Peter's Church Hall; watch repairer; secondhand clothing. The Boys Brigade met at St Peter's Hall; when they paraded in the street they would march blowing their bugles.

I was born in 1911, and my father moved to number 53 Richmond Buildings in 1912. We lived above the newsagent's. We had the shop and an office behind, two bedrooms above, a big living room below the shop, and a kitchen and outside toilet. In the office at the back we did all our booking and took bets, before betting was legal, it was all under the counter, we even took bets off a policeman, and he said unless they had complaints they didn't do anything. We always kept our punters hap-py because in those days it was only sixpences.

My mother and father had four children, and I was the second eldest. Before the First World War, when the third child was born, we moved across the road above the grocer, where he had a double-fronted shop, so our living accommodation was a lot better; we had three bedrooms, an inside toilet and a bathroom. I was in Richmond Buildings from 1912-1939 when I got married and moved to Grove Street. It was lovely living around there, the people were lovely, no trouble at all with anybody (apart from the odd drunk), it was a treat to live there.

My father owned the shop and they only got a small amount of compensation, about £2,000. We had ten morning paperboys, ten evening paperboys; on a Sunday there was my brother, me, my uncle and about eight boys delivering papers; I always helped in the shop. When I left school my father opened another business in Richmond Street, but he closed it when we went into the forces. The shop opened at 5.30 in the morning and stayed open until ten every night, apart from Sunday when he stayed in bed, and only opened at seven in the morning until eight in the evening! We were so busy in our shop, we were one of the biggest newsagents in the town, we delivered over a wide area. When Bill Parr asked his father one day if he could leave work at seven or eight that night, because he had a billiards match, his father said, 'What, do you want two days off a week then?' When I got married I had five days holiday! Our shop stayed open over Bank Holidays and if, for example, Christmas Day fell on a Sunday we would have to deliver the papers. People relied on the newspapers from us for sports results and races because they didn't have television. We gave people things on mace (tick) and they would pay at the end of the week. Gas meters held a penny or a shilling and when we went to the bank we always used to collect five pounds worth of shillings, because people were always coming into our shop and asking for change.

Richmond Buildings: (Hanover) looking north

45

They were wonderful days. We used to play football in the street. We also used to play rounders, kick the bucket, marbles and cards. The old horse-drawn dustmen came, they would go downstairs to pick your dustbin up from your yard outside, empty it in a bin and would even put it back downstairs again. We also had street parties with plenty of food. When we were older we also went down to the beach, if it was warm, at ten o'clock at night. We would collect all the rubbish we could, go into the sea, then set light to the paper and dry ourselves by the fire afterwards.

We had fishermen coming through the streets every morning selling fish, ice cream sellers, people with barrows; muffin and crumpet sellers coming round on a Sunday afternoon ringing a bell. On Sunday morning men would come round with a barrow selling winkles. Tamplin's stables was in Albion Street and they had lovely shire horses. Every street in Brighton had corner shops, and pubs were two a penny! In our area in Richmond Buildings there were at least a dozen public houses. My father used to have a wireless and our customers used to come into the shop to listen to it in the twenties or thirties.

The holiday makers lodged in the houses around this area and they would come back each year and remember us as newsagents. There was poverty around this area. The houses in Richmond Buildings were habitable, we didn't have gardens, just backyards which were very small, but at Mr Parr's we had a greenhouse where we grew tomatoes. The houses were knocked down in 1959 and we moved out in 1958. We knew about it some months beforehand, there was no argument. A lot of people were really unhappy about moving and would have rather have stayed there. The businesses were given some compensation, but not a lot.

Lesley Croydon

We moved to Brighton from London in 1935, when my father bought a small sweet and tobacco shop in Richmond Buildings. He had hoped to be able to run this and make a living but unfortunately he was 'sold a pup', as the previous owner had falsified the books, and he subsequently had to find a job at the 'Home and Colonial' in Gardner Street, leaving the running of the shop to my mother. My mother was rather appalled at the location, as she had not seen the premises before we moved, and said that had she done so she would never have come. Although she had lived in Campbell Road in Brighton from 1916-1923, she had no knowledge of the myriad streets to the east of St Peter's Church.

Richmond Buildings consisted of some small houses and small businesses, almost in equal number. On the eastern corner of Richmond Buildings and Richmond Street was the Lennox Arms Public House; moving northwards there was Gates the wood merchants. They always had 3 barrows of various sizes standing in the street, which we children loved to play on, and while the yard was open there was the continuous background noise of saws and planes.

At number 19 lived a large family who kept greyhounds, mother said they were gypsies. Their living accommodation seemed to be over a large barn or stable. At number 20 a family who were on the parish. Farther up was Parrs the grocer, a small haberdasher, a barber's shop, a sweet and tobacconist, fish and chip shop (fish tuppence and thruppence, chips a penny, scraps a ha'penny), and an undertaker. Number 22 was a curious house as it had a big yard at the side, which I now realise must have originally been for a horse and cart; number 23 was a small electrical shop; number 24 a secondhand shop. On a corner was the sweep, another large family. Next to these houses was the enormous St Peter's Church Hall, which stretched through to Albion Cottages. Several houses below this was Croydon's the newsagent, then some more houses, then a grocer, another grocer, a butcher, a small haberdasher where the husband of the shopkeeper worked as a tailor. The next shop was I believe a shoe repairer, then a hairdresser, then a laundry receiving office (Gochers) and finally a ham and beef shop.

Mr Easen came round every day with his barrow of fruit and vegetables and Mr Sullivan twice a week with a barrow of fresh fish. Milk was delivered by James' dairy in Richmond Street. There was Gigins bread shop in Richmond Street; just round the corner in Albion Hill was a baker who made his own bread. So you can see we did not need to go far for any of our daily needs. A radio shop in Richmond Street charged wireless accumulators for a penny a week, usually on Saturdays. The lamplighter came on his bike to light up.

There was no traffic, other than bicycles, and the children played freely in the streets at all times of the year. We even played out in the darkness of early winter evenings, with no fear of anything or anybody whatsoever. Games were played according to season: tops, hoops, skipping (girls only), hopscotch, marbles, cigarette cards, He, I spy, What's the time Mr Wolf? and roller skating, much to the annoyance of mothers with young babies.

All the children aged between seven and eleven went to Hanover Terrace School (closed in 1939 and never reopened as a school). The hours were nine to twelve and two to four thirty; two hours for dinner and every child went home. During the morning we had a third of a pint of milk each day for a ha'penny, the bottles had cardboard tops and the straws were real straws. We were allowed to take biscuits or sandwiches to have with our milk.

Most of the children went to St Peter's Sunday School which met in the Memorial Hall York Place, or the Sunday School at Ebenezer Baptist Chapel in Ashton Street. The girls joined St Peter's Brownies which met in the church hall. There were occasional excursions to the playground at the Level and to the beach in the summer. The Court Cinema in New Road had films for children on Saturday mornings and we were served the usual diet of Westerns, cartoons, Laurel and Hardy and also had to learn and sing the Gracie Field's Highway Code song: 'Look to the left and look to the right and you'll never, never get run over!'

N W Langridge

We lived in the middle of Richmond Buildings (number 18 or 20) in one of those dingy dark little basement houses with a funny little backyard. There was a little shop next door, a general store, and the lady was really good. I can remember the smell of the loose tea, the spices, humbugs in the jars when she took the lid off, and the Oxo cubes which my brother and I used to eat. A little way down the road from her was a shoe repair shop and we used to go there and watch the cobbler doing his repairs, which was good because the leather smelt beautiful. Down the bottom of the street was a pub where all the Mums and Dads used to meet. We could go down and wait outside and get our big penny or twopenny biscuit. It was a friendly place.

Mrs Goodwin

I was born at 53 Richmond Buildings on 3rd August 1935 and I lived there with my parents until I was four years old. The flat was above and below my grandfather's newsagents shop (Henry Croydon) and my father and uncle both worked for him.

When I married, in 1956, I went back to live in the flat with my husband. It was our first home and consisted of a kitchen, and a dining room cum lounge with an open fireplace in it. The window looked up into the street with a grating over it. There was a little backyard with an outside toilet. To get to our bedroom we had to go up a flight of stairs, through my grandfather's office, up another flight of stairs and we had the front bedroom. When I had my first son I took him back to Richmond Buildings and we moved when he was 8 months old. I lived there for two years before we were moved for the redevelopment of the area.

During the time we were there a lot of the shops were closing down. I can remember the sweep at the end of the road and of course the brewery. When I was pregnant the smell from the brewery used to make me feel sick. There weren't an awful lot of shops open but there were still people in the houses and my grandfather's shop was still a very thriving business, still supporting my uncle and father.

The council offered us a one bedroom flat when it was time to close us down, but we already had one child and we thought that this would be too small. My grandfather must have received compensation for the shop, it was one of the last to close, but it left my uncle and father out of work. My father was fifty when the shop closed and it would have been difficult to obtain another job at his age. My parents set themselves up in another newsagent's business on the corner of Jersey Street with the help of a loan. They offered us the flat over the shop which had two bedrooms, so we took that instead of the council flat. My grandfather retired after the shop closed, he didn't live very long after that.

A lot of old people didn't want to go from the area, but for us it was another step up to a bigger flat. It caused a lot of upset in our family though. My little flat was very cosy and warm, my auntie had lived in it before me and I believe the shop had been in the family for several generations. We would probably still be there if it hadn't been pulled down. The area became very run down towards the end and many houses were boarded up. It was rather lonely, especially when I walked home at night, and it became a bit depressing when my husband went away to do his National Service. I didn't ever work in the shop but I used to do a paper round when I was young, if any of the boys didn't turn up.

Margaret Knight

My Uncle Mark used to live in Cambridge Street. He had a fish barrow which he wheeled around the streets, selling fish he bought at the fish market or that he had caught himself.

My Auntie Alice lived next door to the pub on the corner of Cambridge Street. She brought up twelve children there. In those days kids could play in the streets without any worries, there was always someone to keep an eye on them. Everyone knew each other round this way; you could always borrow things from neighbours even when things were short after the war, and no one took advantage. Day or night you never locked the door.

One thing I notice is that all the small shops have gone. There used to be so many, one or two in every street. Richmond Buildings was full of them, good shops they were; amongst them Mrs Way's fish shop and Archer's the butcher. There was also Halliday's the garment shop and Croucher's the newsagent, all in Richmond Buildings; the undertaker, Sinden's, next door to the furniture shop; oh yes, and a hairdresser for men and women, very amusing in those days; the chimney sweep had a house down there. Albion Street was nearly all cottages owned by the brewery (Tamplins). You could smell the chimney all over the area, horrible it was, the smell of hops burning. You knew it was going to rain when that smell came up the hill from the brewery. I can remember that Gates the builder also had a place down there, I used to go and play snooker there sometimes, then it moved to Coleman Street.

All these streets were cleaner than streets are today. People would never leave their rubbish on the pavement for days like they do now, and no one would have been without nets and curtains in the windows like youngsters do around here now. Even in the streets that were supposed to be poor ones, the houses were much smarter than today. No cars of course, it was strange to see one parked in this area, the streets seemed quite big then.

You could tell the time by the hooters going off at the stations or factories around the town.

Mr & Mrs Moore

In Richmond Buildings was a working men's club which seemed to play a large part in local social life. A saw mill stood at the Richmond Street end. Several small shops made a living; the Croydon family had a busy paper shop there. When I look back I think that some of the houses in that area, particularly in Claremont Street, were very fine, and I sometimes wonder who deemed in the thirties that these properties should go. Although I still live in this area, things will never be the same, I believe it's called progress, but people, especially the older ones, don't think there is the same spirit of close friendships these days.

Robert Cristofoli

I was staying in Cannon Street in 1928 with my sister's husband and parents, a Mr and Mrs Virgo who were very well known. He had a boat on the beach which took people for rides on the sea, he also went fishing and sold cockles and shrimps from this boat. My stepfather had a bootmakers shop in Richmond Buildings. He was very well known as his father before him started the business, they made boots and shoes of all kinds right from the soles. The short time I was home I used to go to the 'Friends' leather shop for steel pelts, wax thread, and leather cuttings. The shop was small.

When I lived in the area I used to walk right up Richmond Hill, to Dinapore Street, to deliver repairs.

Winifred Evento

Ivory Place

I was born at my paternal grandmother's house in Sussex Terrace on Christmas Eve 1925. I lived there with my parents and sister who was ten years old at the time. She tells me the house was full of assorted aunts, uncles and cousins; we occupied one room. Space was at such a premium that my cot was in fact the bottom drawer of a chest of drawers. She saved me from suffocation, when somebody closed the draw, inadvertently, with me in it.

My grandmother had a secondhand clothes shop in Edward Street, as well as a fruit and vegetable stall in Upper Gardner Street on a Saturday, where my sister had to help out. My paternal grandfather was dead by now so these enterprises were her main sources of income.

When I was around twelve months of age we moved to my maternal grandparents' house in Ivory Place. My grandfather was a fisherman; fisherfolk families in those days were invariably large and it was not uncommon for uncles, cousins, and nephews to have the same Christian names. Therefore for identification purposes nicknames (which usually referred to an individual's physical appearance) were used.

The living to be earned from fishing in those days was precarious to say the least. Fishermen were away from home much of the time, because it was the practice to follow the herring and mackerel shoals as they moved down the Channel, and land the catches wherever, until it was time to return to Brighton. In the meantime the fishermen's families had been living on credit, sometimes the earnings only just covered the credit. My grandfather eventually gave up fishing and became a coach painter at Lancing Carriage works. The house in Ivory Place may be one of those shown in the photograph.

Eventually we moved to a house of our own in Albion Cottages, an L shaped alley with one end in Albion Hill and one in Albion Street. There was a row of houses on the eastern side of the alley, with a general yard at the northern end and Tamplins' Brewery stables at the southern end, the backyard walls of Albion Street on the western end. I lived there until I was ten, when our house was condemned we moved into Manor Farm in March 1936. The whole of Albion Cottages was not condemned at this time, only our house and the house next door. The remaining houses were refurbished and were not demolished until I think around 1960.

There was a community spirit, engendered of course by the fact of all being in the same boat. Certainly for us children it was obligatory that the elder children looked after the younger ones when we went to the beach, or to the Race Hill for the day, packed off with a bottle of made up lemonade and sandwiches. Unlike some, I cannot say that I look back on those days with any affection. The memories I have are of being damned cold in winter, suffering chilblained ears which bled, having rickets through my poor diet and certainly not being over protected by my parents.

The house in Albion Cottages consisted of a small front yard behind a stone wall, two rooms downstairs, one a kitchen cum living room, the other a scullery containing a copper and a sink. At the back was a small yard with an outside toilet and in the centre a surface water drain; much excitement was caused one day when the old lady next door fell down drunk and got her head stuck in the open drain, but she was eventually freed. Upstairs in the house were two small bedrooms.

Ivory Place: (Hanover) looking north

Mondays in those days was always washday, and because of the narrowness of the street, clothes lines were slung from the front of the houses across the street to the wall opposite. Woe betide any youngster who accidentally brushed against the washing as he ducked beneath it to get to or from his home. The old lady next door (who had stuck her head in the drain) managed to set fire to her chimney, a common occurrence in those days, and the fire brigade was sent for. As the street was so narrow, it was impossible to get the fire engine into the street, so it was necessary to run hoses from a fire hydrant at the same time the children of the street were arriving home for dinner. The combination of sweating, struggling, swearing firemen, kids yelling and generally skylarking, irate housewives berating the firemen while they struggled to get their washing in, whilst a black ball of soot and smoke settled over all. It looked like something from Bedlam.

A weekly event in Albion Cottages took place every Sunday afternoon, this was a visit by the Salvation Army band from Congress Hall. This, I think, was directly due to my father, his half brother was a member of the band. An annual event which took place was the decorating of the horses and carts of Tamplins' Brewery; the horses were bedecked with bells, ribbons and brasses and the carts were immaculately polished.

Sickness was a do it yourself affair, or a visit to the herbalist, sending for the doctor was unheard of because nobody could afford it. There were two herbalists who were patronised by the street, one by the name of Stokes, who had his establishment at the corner of Waterloo Place and Phoenix Place, the other at the Open Market at the London Road entrance. When I was diagnosed by my mother as having mumps or swollen glands, she took me to the Open Market herbalist who concocted some black ointment to be applied once a day and I was cured. Whether this was due to the ointment or nature I wouldn't like to say.

Children in those days were all expected to run errands regularly as a matter of course. In winter we could not afford to buy coal by the hundredweight, we used to purchase it in fourteen pound paper bags and it was one of my errands to go to the shop in Richmond Buildings, which was the street above, and buy a bag of coal and carry it home. Every dinner time I fetched a bottle of Guinness for a neighbour from the pub at the bottom of Albion Hill. My reward was the halfpenny deposit on the returned empty bottle, whether the sale of alcohol to a nine year old was illegal or not I do not know.

My final errand was to walk to J.J. Sears the grocer in Preston Road every Saturday morning to buy three pennyworth of pieces of bacon for a bacon pudding, a Saturday treat. The buying of rashers was rare, porridge was our staple diet. Another regular item in our diet was rabbit which I didn't like very much. It meant that after Mother skinned the rabbit I was wanted to take the skin to a rag and bone merchant's in Peacehaven Street, where I would receive the sum of one penny, which was not for me but had to be taken back to mother.

The rag and bone shop was a dark and gloomy place, what couldn't be seen was best left to the imagination. Recalling Richmond Buildings it is true to say the shops there provided most things for every day living. I recall two grocers, a greengrocer, a newsagent, a barber, a sweep, a cat's meat shop, a fish and chip shop, a shoe repairer, a pub, St Peter's Church Hall and finally an undertaker.

It was March 1936 when we were rehoused in a brand new council house in Manor Road, Manor Farm, a house that was comparatively a palace. I remember we put our few bits and pieces on an open lorry and climbed on afterwards. I left without a backward glance. I'm not sure that my parents were too sad because friends and relatives from nearby streets were also destined to move to Manor Farm, so the old community spirit to some extent would be re-established.

Mr W.G. Holmes

The houses next to mine were knocked down. There was a little row of houses that had quite nice gardens, then more houses where the rooms weren't very big, then the road went up to a builder's yard, where Ivory Place narrowed, and at the Richmond Hill end there were six or seven houses which had very long gardens.

On the other corner coming down from Richmond Street, the Grand Parade side, at the top corner there was an upholsterer's, which was all knocked down for the widening of the road. It was a very long building, opposite Richmond Buildings, then there were a row of terraced houses opposite the builder's yard.

I remember the Council houses that were built before the war, in 1935, and they are still there. They were basement and two up houses, and on the corner was a big shop. They had demolished the older houses to put them up. They were quite good looking terraced houses.

My grandmother lived in the house; it had a nice garden at the back, and on today's standards it would be good, with a small garden at the front. It was a very narrow street, with a small pavement.

The school clinic was already built and the chest clinic, on the corner of Sussex Street, now Morley Street.

During the war, the school clinic was hit by a bomb and my grandmother was sitting in her living room when the plaster came on top of her, and there were also marks on the wall where a fighter came low and put bullets in the wall.

The rooms in the house were small, the staircase was narrow. There was an alleyway up the side with a big gate which you went through to get to the yard, a nice size yard, where my grandmother used to keep her mangle, then there were some steps that went up to a garden from the yard. On modern standards for a town house it was quite a lot of garden. They used to have a shed in the garden. There was a big wall at the back. There was a lot of space outside, but the rooms were very small, and ridden with bugs. It was old plaster. She didn't own it.

My grandmother used the front room as her bedroom, and she used to have masses of seaside ornaments. There was a table in front of the window, a fireplace which was cleaned and polished up. She didn't have a great deal of room.

Upstairs, there was a narrow staircase with two rooms, a small bedroom at the back and a large bedroom at the front. I had the back bedroom. The room was more or less plain. There were fireplaces in the bedrooms. We had a lodger occasionally living in the upstairs front bedroom. It had wallpaper and a fire, but I don't think any of the fires in the bedrooms were used. We used to use the dining room, which was more or less the kitchen as well; you would do your washing up in the scullery. In the scullery there was a big earthenware sink. We used to listen to the radio, but we used to go out a lot, you would make your own entertainment, unlike youngsters today, where television is laid on for them. I used to walk up to Race Hill to play football or go to the pictures, kids used to play football or cricket on the Level.

We did have a tin bath but we used to go to North Road once a week. They were big baths. We sometimes used the bath, using a copper to boil the water up and tip it in the bath. And we would use the copper to heat the clothes and put them through the mangle.

There weren't many people of my age. I started work at 14. I worked in for a baker and I used to push a bread cart all the way up Dyke Road and deliver in the Hove area. I didn't have much education to speak of because we weren't well off.

The milk cart used to come down the road, still horse drawn, and there were still a few motor cars around.

There was a pub in Richmond Street near Saunders Glass, where it had a tiny Jug and Bottle department, where I would buy my grandmother stout for her rheumatism.

Mr Tullett

I lived in Ivory Place and went to Circus Street school, which is still there. I did not live with my parents as my mother left us during 1914-1918. As we were very poor I can't remember having any new clothes until I left school and started work.

We lived next door to Mrs Gunn who used to sit outside Hanningtons selling violets, and the family are florists now. The muffin man used to come around every Sunday morning. It was a very friendly street.

My sister lived in Carlton Row near the herring dees (where the herring was smoked). I remember seeing the children come sliding down the hill (Sussex Street) on tin trays when the snow was on the ground.

They were funny little houses. We had to whiten the door step every day. We had an outside wash house, where we used to have a fire under the copper to boil the clothes every Monday morning.

L Boyle

Ashton Street

I moved to Ashton Street when I was about six years old, because a bomb damaged our other house. I went to Richmond Street School at the bottom of Richmond Street; my headmistress was Miss Coombes. Her sister used to give us talks in the Ebenezer Chapel on the corner of Ashton Street on Sunday and Tuesday evenings; we would have a bible class and lantern shows. The lantern shows were mainly missionary and travel slides, entertaining rather than brainwashing; I enjoyed going funnily enough. We had school treats, but I didn't usually go because I used to play up a lot, I was the troublemaker. The chapel is now where Ivory Place was, they moved all the bodies buried there to the cemetery at Bear Road.

When we moved to Ashton Street the top part of the road was bomb damaged. Nearly all the houses were occupied, except number 18, I think, was empty, because we used to think it was haunted.

The people of Ashton Street were very friendly, and one of the things that amazes me was that at that time I can't remember anyone locking their door. If the door knocker went we either thought it was the rent man or we're in trouble, because everybody else would automatically open the door and call in, some of them would just walk in! If it rained people used to put their aspidistras out on the pavement next to the dustbins, for a watering.

We lived at number 39 Ashton Street on the side farthest away from St Peter's Church. We had three bedrooms, but really we only used two, the other one my grandmother used to call a slip room, others would call it a box room. I lived with my grandmother and mother whilst my Dad was away at war and we didn't use the other room until the others got back. The ground floor of the house was the old Victorian style with the passage, the sitting room where no-one was allowed to go, and a room behind it where we lived and cooked on the old black range. Out at the back was a scullery with one of the old yellow stone sinks, with a copper in the corner. We had gas for cooking and electric lighting, and at the back was a little yard. You always thought if any of your friends lived in houses with bay windows they were ever so rich.

There weren't any shops in Ashton Street, though there was one on the bottom corner, but it was always shut up. It was full of furniture but no-one seemed to live there. My mum did her shopping at the top of Ashton Street until they were bombed. On the corner of Liverpool Street was a grocer called Pudney's, where she would go to get her groceries once a week; but she would walk down to the London Road and through the market daily. We didn't go to the Western Road, that was an outing if you wanted something special.

In the late 1940's the rent for our house in Ashton Street was seventeen shillings and a penny and there was a hell of a row when it went up to seventeen and four pence, I can remember how annoyed my grandmother was. We paid the rent to a private landlord. I think only one woman in the whole street owned her house.

There were quite a few children in Ashton Street, and we played in the street most of the time, there was no traffic about. It was funny when my mate's elder sister was courting, because her boyfriend had a car and when he came to pick her up on Sundays we would all line up across the road to see the car.

I have good memories of Ashton Street, we were close, and if anyone was ill

everyone used to come in and help one another. I think it was because we were all in the same boat. I remember the new National Health Service in 1948, because I went down with scarlet fever, and I remember my grandmother saying it's lucky the Health Service is here, otherwise we would have to pay for the doctor. I always remember being confined to the house, in a room on my own, with a thick blanket over the door with some carbolic on it or something. My grandmother looked after me as my Mum went out to work full-time. I never came home to an empty house and still can't get used to it now.

I left Richmond Street School at about seven and went to Finsbury Road School until I was eleven. There was a Catholic school opposite us at Finsbury Road, run by nuns, and we used to see them walking out occasionally in long crocodiles. I was the only one in my class to pass the eleven-plus at Finsbury Road, but I didn't want to go to the grammar school because all my mates wouldn't be going, and because of the price of the uniform, which was too much for my Mum to afford. So I went to Fawcett, opposite St Peter's Church with my friends, I got a good education there and had no regrets at not going to the grammar school.

The social life was good in Ashton Street. We used to go blackberry picking at Patcham on Sweet Hill off the London Road, get a big basket full, then go down to the open market and they'd buy them off you.

At the top of Ashton Street was the baker and Mr Martin delivered the milk. I remember getting lifts in his barrow as a child with the empties. Our evenings were spent on the street, or wandering around the Level. We made our own entertainment. As children we played chalk games such as hopscotch and spiral chalk games. I had a ball just bigger than a tennis ball, which we played football with in Circus Street. We also used to build bonfires in the street, mainly in Cambridge Street where we played a lot; one side was a bomb site, where we played before the prefabs were built. The police were very good; we were always in trouble for pinching apples, but the respect for the police was much better and they had a different attitude then; a clip round the ear and 'I'll be round to tell your father' was enough. You were slightly terrified of them.

My Gran used to do washing over the sink and Monday morning you got out of the house as quickly as possible, otherwise you got lumbered with the job of winding the mangle. She boiled the water up on the stove and washed in the sink. In other houses, where the housewives were younger, they had machines, but Gran was set in her ways.

We had our main meal in the middle of the day, and on Sundays we always had a sit down meal at twelve o'clock. It was a bit of a nuisance, because my friends would have theirs at different times, according to whether their parents went to the pub or not. So on Sundays we couldn't go out in the morning and we couldn't go out in the afternoon. We had a radio, (we listened to Radio Luxembourg and my Gran and Mum listened to Housewife's Choice) but no television until the Coronation in 1952, and by then there were six televisions in the street. We had a beautiful gramophone as well.

The trades of the men in Ashton Street were engineering, railway works, painters and decorators. We had a chocolate maker in our street too.

Ashton Street: (Hanover) looking north

We had a Morrison shelter in the back room and it took up nearly all the room. We had a tin bath. Our diet was basic, with rationing after the war, but we got by; everyone got by because they knew someone who could get things on the black market. My Mum was OK working at the Red Shield club, and a woman around the corner kept chickens and would let you have eggs if you needed them.

Trafalgar Street was where we bought our suits in the Fifties. There were lots of tailors up and down the street, such as Sammy Gordon's, and they used to drag you in off the street to try suits on, and if you thought it didn't fit they would hold it in at the back! But anyone who was anyone had their suits made up there. It took hours looking at the cloth and then deciding on the style, size of the lapels and whether you would have two or three pockets. You would often go back two or three times for fittings. I had a friend whose father had a tailor's shop in Bond Street and I bought three or four suits off him at a discount for about £7.

My Gran felt terrible about moving from Ashton Street to Hollingdean, she was always moaning, 'I'm going to die in this new house, I know.' I left Ashton Street in 1956 to join the army and the family moved out in about 1957.

Alan Jeal

Ashton Street is typical of streets in the Albion Hill area, many of which still remain. The majority of the houses in the area would have been rented at this time, but since then a considerable change in tenure has taken place and they are now mainly owner occupied and kept in better state of repair as a result. The Environmental Health Department promoted improvement grants after the last clearances were completed, and tenure changes had taken place. Elderly people were renting the houses, when they died younger people bought them.

Features displayed by the photograph show a predominance of basements on both sides of the terrace; they are effectively three storey buildings running up the hillside. The basements on the right hand side would have been poorer because of the incline on the left, particularly at the rear, and there are some features of disrepair; doorways again open straight onto the pavement.

There is a problem with refuse storage; residents would have had to bring the rubbish right through the houses from the back to the front for collection. This is still the case though the problem has been made worse as a result of many houses being converted to flats. The planners did not look too hard at facilities and the consequences for refuse of conversion to flats; when the flats were sold the leaseholders complained of rubbish dumping in their basement areas.

Paul Eardley : Environmental Health Officer

Claremont Street

My mother moved to Claremont Street from Centurion Road in 1942 or '43, when I was four or five. I lived there with my mother, a sister and brother, then after the war my younger sister was born there. I went to the school in Richmond Street, which was round the corner from Claremont Street. You didn't need anyone to take you to school, as there were no cars. The school had a lovely smell, they used to wax the floors. We used to have to go into the air raid shelters, which were in the playground. We were given exercise books that had been cut in half or into three, and we had to draw or sing while we were down there. We were given big thick pencils to use, and we always sang hymns. My brother was in the baby class, and he had to go to bed in the afternoon on a little camp bed, he hated that.

My father was in the army at the time, and my mother didn't work; my father wouldn't allow her to, she just looked after us. I remember we had a Morrison shelter in 32 Claremont Street, we used to sleep there every night, and my mother would give us each a photograph of our father. When he returned, either my brother or I said 'only one?' We thought that as we had one photograph each we would have one father each! We slept in the shelter for as long as I can remember. My mother and grandmother had a mattress on top of the shelter, and if the warning went off they went inside the shelter with us. We had bicycle lamps inside.

The house was terraced, with a front room which nobody went into; it was kept clean and dusted, and we only went in there when we had visitors or at Christmas. We had a long passageway, quite dark, and the room behind that we always called the kitchen, which was really our living room, where we ate and listened to the radio. Then there was a scullery with the sink, cooker and an old fashioned brick built copper, though Mum never used that. We had a backyard with a toilet and our bath hung on the wall. We had baths in front of the fire; only one a week (it would be youngest first) without changing the water, so I got everybody else's dirty water. My mother would say that the youngest was the cleanest, my brother used to go before me and I remember saying 'Don't wee in the water'. He would get out and say 'I've weed in the water', and I used to think it was heaven to have a bath before anyone else.

Upstairs there were two quite big bedrooms and a room which was called the slip room, just a small bedroom. Everybody in the street called it by that name. We had a bad problem with mice, we had a cat that used to catch mice, but we also had to have traps down. My mother only paid about a pound a week in rent. There was nothing nice about the house at all, the nicest thing about the street was the people.

My mother used to sit on the front doorstep. One side of the street had doorsteps and the other side came straight onto the pavement; those who didn't have a step would cross over and sit on our doorstep. In the evening groups of mothers used to sit on a doorstep and talk. They had this friendship in the street where everyone would help each other. There were an awful lot of women who had children, but whose husbands were away in the war, so everyone helped each other and all the kids played together. You hardly ever saw a car, and you would get upset if you had to stop what you were doing for a car to go by. We could play hopscotch and it would stay until it rained. There was no fear of cars, they didn't go fast. A lot of us who were kids are still great friends now, everybody knew each other. If someone was having a baby the other mothers would help out. I used to go shopping for people.

Babies would be left outside in their prams, without any worries, and we would push them from one lamp post to the next; we didn't have a choice, we did as we were told.

In Claremont Row they built prefabs, and these prefabs were wonderful. We lived in these old houses, but the prefabs had bathrooms and a fridge, they were lovely, they were modern compared with our house. The toilets were inside, and they had a bathroom, they were so light and airy. There were only about six prefabs there, I think there were some in Cambridge Street as well.

My mother moved out in 1958, as a result of the slum clearance. She used to write to me saying that she was hoping she could move soon, because by now the houses were in a bad state, she really wanted to move.

She was moved to Moulsecoomb. She hated it there because she had none of her old neighbours with her, they were all moved to different areas. Everyone wanted to move because the houses which most people rented were bad, and the majority were moved to council property. The house in Moulsecoomb was much nicer, but my mother missed all her friends. In the war years the association was so close, they looked after each other and checked if you were OK. If you needed a doctor, someone would make sure you had a shilling to pay the doctor.

My brother and sister were very pleased when they moved, but when they were living in Moulsecoomb they couldn't walk home, they suddenly had to remember to get the last bus. They missed being in the centre of the city. Most of all they missed their friends, although they kept in contact, they were often far away. My sister used to say it was always a nuisance, if you went to the Regent dancing, you couldn't walk home anymore, you had to get the last bus. My father was quite happy to move, but, like my mother, he missed the people he knew. He was a bus driver after the war, he used to drive the trolley buses.

We thought Claremont Street was the best street. Nowadays it would be pretty awful, but it was one of the friendliest places. My mother used to say about Moulsecoomb, 'You could die out here and no one would know'. My mother got Moulsecoomb and my aunt, who lived opposite, got Woodingdean. They weren't kept together, they didn't put any thought into it at all. It may have depended on the number of children you had and the size of the house you needed.

Mrs Jackson

This street fascinated me as a child, because of the wall and railings which crossed from Claremont Street to Dinapore Street across Richmond Street, to stop the horses slipping down the hill. There were some real characters in Claremont Street, I remember a lady we called 'Fluffy Flo'.

Robert Cristofoli

Claremont Street: (Hanover) rear of west side looking north

Albion Street

Thomas Packham, my great great grandfather, was living at 7 Albion Street in 1839 when it was a drayman's store belonging to Tamplin's Brewery. He had arrived some ten years earlier from Lewes with a sack on his back and eleven pence in his pocket, hoping to make a better living in Brighton. He was an ostler by trade; so 'being good with horses' he probably found work with the brewery while his wife Mary took in washing, the staple back street Brighton industry of that time.

By 1851 the family had moved to Number 4 Albion Street which still exists; and Thomas would doubtless have been astonished to learn that the house next door was up for sale recently for nearly £74,000 and described as 'a charming Victorian terraced two bedroom house with small patio'. Thomas would have known the patio as a backyard where his wife hung out the washing and laboured over the tub on sunny days. The rest of the washing would have been strung across the street. Harriet, his daughter aged twenty-two, did 'flat trimming', while sixteen year old Eliza helped with the ironing. Young Charlotte, aged fourteen was a nursemaid.

Others in the family still living at home were Alfred, Frederick and George, who was my great grandfather, and then attending school. The family budget would have been tight, particularly as there was yet another addition to the table: grandson William, the child of the unmarried Harriet who had moved from Foundry Street to live with mother. Sadly Thomas from Wadhurst, where he was born in 1790, never made his fortune in Brighton. He lived for a while at 3 Richmond Buildings with his daughter Harriet, when she married William Grainger. He must have been an easy going character, because not only did he give his father-in-law a home, but also Harriet's brother Frederick and her child William. Thomas senior finished his days in the old Brighton Workhouse in Dyke Road.

Maurice Packham

TOWNSHIP OF FLATS ON THE HILL, START ON BIG PLAN THIS YEAR?

The first stage in the creation of a pleasant vista from the Queen's Park Road ridge down the valley to St Peter's Church is likely to be commenced next September. In the process, a mass of old houses now huddled together will be swept away, and in their place will appear blocks of flats, some of the 'skyscraper' variety. This ambitious transformation plan is comprised in what is known as the Albion Hill redevelopment scheme, which takes in just over 11 acres. On this extremely hilly ground it has been decided to erect 426 dwellings in 'mixed development'; that is to say, in 2, 3, 8 and 11-storey blocks.

The creation of a self-contained community in the heart of modern Brighton is the object in view, for it is intended to incorporate in the new estate shops and social amenities together with provision for religious activities. Club and community centre provision will probably be made possible in semi-basements of the taller buildings. Health-giving open spaces, for so long absent from this close-packed, hilly area, will lead through the estate right up to the ridge of Queen's Park Road. 'By the use of high blocks of flats it has been possible to provide large areas of open space surrounding the blocks, which will be well planted with trees and grass.'

Brighton and Hove Herald 4.1.58

Albion Street: (Hanover) looking north

Ladies Mile Road Patcham

Patcham Parish

At a vestry meeting of the said Parish held the twenty fifth day December one thousand eight hundred and fourteen in pursuance of a Notice given in the Church of the said Parish the twenty fifth day of the said month.

Present	Thomas Scrase	churchwarden
	Thomas Hodson	overseer
	Jn Poole	}
	Josh Harland	} for habitants
	Willm Vine	}

Unanimously resolved by the Inhabitants now present that the Churchwardens and Overseers be authorised to erect and build five Tenements or more if they shall think necessary not exceeding six for the use of the said Parish upon the Ground to be obtained of the Lord of the Manor and that the Expenses of the said buildings be paid out of the Rates to be raised for the Relief of the Poor of the Parish in the manner the said Churchwardens and Overseers may think best for the Parish.

(Sigd)	Thos Scrase	Churchwarden
	Thos Hodson	overseer
	John Poole	
	Joseph Harland	
	Wm Vine	

Parish of Patcham

At a Vestry of the said Parish held the 23d January 1816 in pursuance of a Notice given in the Church of the said parish the 21st inst

Present	Thomas Scrase	Churchwd
	William Tanner	Churchwd
	Thomas Hodson	Overseer
	R B Sandiland	Constable
	William Vine	Headboro'
	Chas Thonbridge	Inhabt

Resolved unanimously that Mr William Tanner who has been admitted to the piece of Ground on which the 5 Cottages are erected in Patcham Drove do make a Conditional Surrender thereof to Mrs Martha and Susannah Hamshar for securing £250 with interest at five per cent the said sum of £250 having been advanced by the said M & S Hamshar at our request for the erection of the said Cottages. And we do hereby agree that the sum of Twelve pounds ten shillings shall be annually paid out of the Poor Rates of the said Parish (over & above the Interest) until the whole of the said Principal & Interest shall be fully paid and discharged.

(Sigd)	Thos Scrase	Churchwarden
	Wm Tanner Jun	Do
	Thos Hodson	Overseer
	R B Sandiland	
	C Thonbridge	
	Wm Vine	

East Sussex Record Office PAR 437/12/1

Ladies Mile Road: front. These cottages still stand, much altered, as Nos. 36-44 Ladies Mile Road

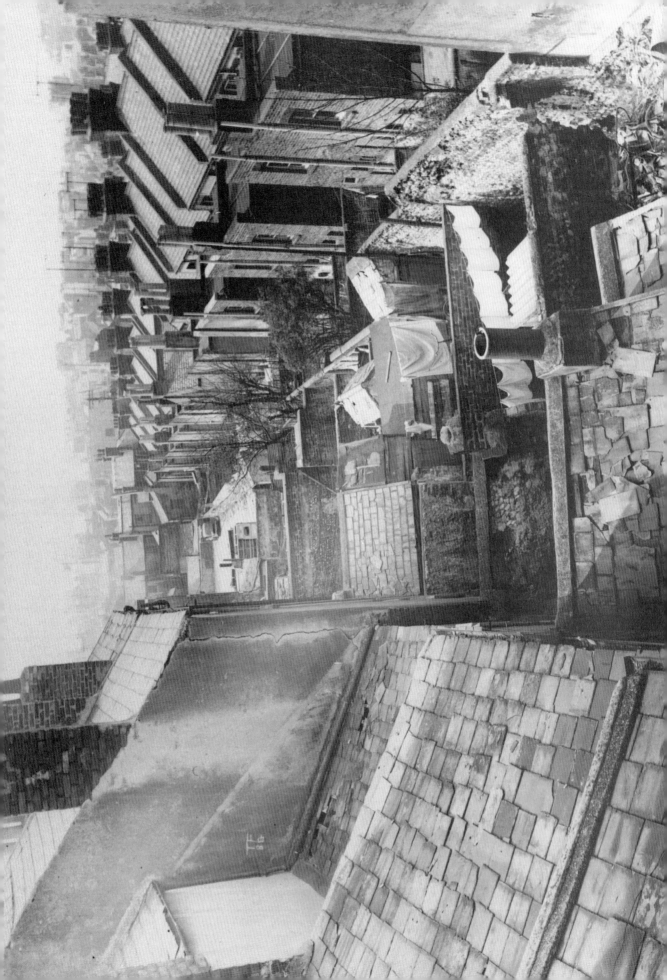

About Back Street Brighton

1st edition

This book was made by: Jayne Tyler, Jacqueline Connatty, Richard Knapp, Georgina Attrell, Michael Hayler, Selma, Alice, Dicon, Piran & Sukey Montford, Peter Messer, Alistair Thompson, Elfrida Oldfield, Denise Francis, Jacky Watts, Paul Eardley and Brighton Borough Council Environmental Health Department.

Photographs: Brighton Borough Council Environmental Health Department.

Published by QueenSpark Books, Basement 68 Grand Parade Brighton and
Lewis Cohen Urban Studies Centre at Brighton Polytechnic 68 Grand Parade Brighton.
October 1989

Copyright: QueenSpark Books & the Lewis Cohen Urban Studies Centre at Brighton Polytechnic.

Printed by Faulwood and Herbert 38A North Road Preston Village Brighton.

ISBN No: 0 904733 25 4

In this edition QueenSpark Books and the Lewis Cohen Urban Studies Centre acknowledged funding from South East Arts and Brighton Borough Council.

The Lewis Cohen Urban Centre at Brighton Polytechnic was an information and resource centre concerned with understanding the local environment. It closed on 31 July 1995.

2nd edition

This book was made possible when *Back Street Brighton*, along with all other QueenSpark books, was OCR scanned for the QueenSpark on-line archive. It is a faithful reproduction of the first edition using today's technology to re-create the original layout.

Some typographic inconsistencies have been corrected and there is less hyphenation of words, but no editing or updating of the original content has been undertaken. The Introduction explaining how the first edition was conceived is the original one.

The photographs taken by Brighton Borough Council Environmental Health Department were scanned and licensed courtesy of The Royal Pavilion and Museums, Brighton & Hove.

Published by QueenSpark Books, Brighton.
November 2007

Copyright: QueenSpark Books and the University of Brighton.

Printed by GH Graphics (Hastings) Ltd.

ISBN No: 9780 904733 37 2

University of Brighton

Grosvenor Street:(between 59 Edward Street and 59 Carlton Hill) backyards

About QueenSpark

For 35 years QueenSpark has been telling the 'unheard stories' of the people of Brighton & Hove and, through the publication of over 80 books, has established itself as a national leader in widening access to publishing.

Involvement with QueenSpark has helped many people achieve creative and personal validation. A large number of our participants have gained skills and experience that has enabled them to find voluntary and paid employment within the literary arts.

Since 2003 QueenSpark has developed into a vibrant, prolific organisation, demonstrated by the co-ordination of four websites:

- www.queensparkbooks.org.uk
- www.20thcenturysparks.org.uk
- www.thedeckchair.org.uk
- www.mybrightonandhove.org.uk

which:

- offer an enhanced awareness of the city's literary practise and heritage
- support the development of local creative and non-fiction literature
- offer individuals the opportunity to publish their work online
- make this literature accessible to students, academics, and a wider audience

QueenSpark Books

In 1989, when *Back Street Brighton* was first launched, QueenSpark had published 20 books, mainly local autobiographies, but also books of poetry, prose, history and politics. Many of them had sold out one or more editions. Some of the most popular books could have sold out many more editions and it is with great pleasure that we can now include a new edition of *Back Street Brighton* amongst our list of books currently in print:

Back Street Brighton - memories and photographs of Brighton in the late forties and early fifties. Price: £10.99

Lost Shops of Brighton - QueenSpark's 2008 calendar featuring previously unseen photographs. Price £6.99

Refuge - stories of survival and escape from migrants visiting The Cowley Club. Price: £5.99

Roofless - a collection of photographs, essays, stories and poems by homeless and ex-homeless people from Brighton. Price: £7.99

Pebble on the Beach - the true story of one boy's ability to survive. Price: £7.99

Alt-Future - a companion work to Alt-History, this is the result of a competition to write creatively about the city's future. Price: £6.99

Bangla Brighton - a series of moving true life accounts of life on the south coast by Brighton and Hove's Bangladeshi community. Price: £5.99

Alt-History - alternative 'histories' of Brighton and Hove from new writers. Price: £4.99

Missing the Nile - a fascinating look at the customs and culture of the Sudanese community in the Brighton and Hove area. Price £5.00

Talking Books - audio CD containing three very different life stories, focussing on and featuring the renowned West Pier in Brighton. Price: £5.00

School Reports - reminiscences and anecdotes from past pupils who attended St. Luke's School, in the Queens Park area of Brighton in the years between 1908 - 1983. Price: £6.99

Remember the First Time? - a diverse collection of childhood memories. Price: £3.00

Are you sitting comfortably? - stories for children. Price: £3.00

International Service - the tale of a young woman's naive teenage years, when her domineering father chose the jobs that she took and discouraged her passion for writing. Price: £4.00